The Gift
of
Faith

Tending the Spiritual Lives
of Children

Jeanne Harrison Nieuwejaar

Skinner House Books
Boston

*The book is dedicated
to the people of the
Community Church of North Orange
and Tully, Massachusetts—
the church of my childhood—
and
to the people of
the Unitarian Universalist Congregation
in Milford, New Hampshire,
who sustain my faith
in the value of religious community.*

First Edition Copyright © 1999, Second Edition Copyright © 2003 by Jeanne Harrison Nieuwejaar. All rights reserved. Published by Skinner House Books. Skinner House Books is an imprint of the Unitarian Universalist Association, a liberal religious organization with more than 1,000 congregations in the U.S. and Canada. 25 Beacon Street, Boston, MA 02108-2800

Printed in Canada.

Cover design: Sue Charles

Text design: WordCrafters

ISBN 1-55896-443-6

Library of Congress Cataloging-in-Publication Data
Nieuwejaar, Jeanne Harrison, 1944–
    The gift of faith : tending the spiritual lives of children / Jeanne Harrison Nieuwejaar — 2nd ed.
      p. cm.
    Includes bibliographical references (p.).
    ISBN 1-55896-443-6
    1. Christian education of children. 2. Christian education—Home training. I. Title.
    BV1590.N54 2003
    268′.432—dc21   2002029441

05
10 9 8 7 6 5 4 3 2

Contents

~

Preface to
the Second Edition

~

In the weeks following September 11, 2001, that fresh blue-sky day when planes crashed into tall buildings and our world was changed forever, churches and synagogues were filled to overflowing. People were in need of solace; they felt at sea and sought an anchor; in the midst of chaos and despair they sought hope and meaning. Adults sought it for themselves. Parents sought it both for themselves and for their children. It was a desperate time.

And the religious communities responded prodigiously. They offered candlelight vigils, prayer services, memorial services, bereavement groups, counseling, peer support, messages that helped worshippers to sort through the confusing strands of fear, anger, vengeance, and grief. They sponsored blood drives and victim relief funds, interfaith connections and dialogue, and education about the Muslim faith. In that awful time of crisis, the need for spiritual sustenance surfaced in people who hadn't been to a church or temple for decades, as well as in regular churchgoers. And in the midst of that trauma, even as we acknowledged all that had been lost or called into question, we also counted our blessings.

Folks who were part of a religious community could count among their blessings that they knew where to go for spiritual support in those awful days. Those who had a religious home could go to a familiar place where they were known and where the language and rituals were known to them. Those unconnected to a religious community, although I am sure they were welcomed into the places of worship to which they flocked, did not have that extra measure of familiarity.

Added to all the other insecurities of that time, they perhaps did not know where to go, what time the services might be, or even how to get that information. They may not have known where to park, which entrance to use, how to dress, or how to behave in the rituals of the community. All of these are little things, but in times of great stress and vulnerability, they add to the feelings of uncertainty, of insecurity, of being unprotected. On a deeper level, those just entering a house of worship for the first time in years may have found themselves unwittingly in religious communities whose particular theology and language were not consistent with their personal faith.

How blessed were those who could go unthinkingly to a place where they could simply rest in the embrace of a familiar spirituality, supported by a beloved community of fellow worshippers. How blessed were such parents. How blessed were their children.

In writing the first edition of *The Gift of Faith*, I hoped to help parents to understand what a deep and lasting gift a grounding in faith would be for their children and to see how their regular participation in a religious community was an integral component of that gift. That writing was done in 1997 and 1998, a time of national peace and security—unlike today. But, of course, quite apart from the larger political world, our personal lives are constantly in flux. Families in every era, on every day, are vulnerable to the tragedies of life.

On any fresh, blue-sky day, a tragic fire can flare, a terminal illness can be diagnosed, a family secret can creep out of the closet, a car can crash. On any day a family can be in need of a sustaining faith and a spiritual community for support, solace, and hope. How blessed are those who have a faith that is clear and grounded. How blessed are those who have a vocabulary for expressing that faith and a way of prayer that is meaningful. How blessed are those who have a religious community.

Jeanne Harrison Nieuwejaar
New York

Prologue

~

The church of my small-town, New England childhood was literally across the street from my home and was a powerful part of my growing up. I saw it from my living room window, played on its steps, heard its bell on Sunday mornings, and freely came and went through its doors throughout the week. Its smells, its light, its people are deeply embedded within me. This was a community church, attended by almost all of the churchgoing residents of the village. The social, spiritual, and business lives of these people were intertwined in an organic way which I then took for granted but now see as rare.

My spiritual life as a child was also organic, experienced not as something distinct and separate, but integrated into all phases of my living. I also took this for granted then and now see it as rare. The church was no small part of that integrated spirituality, its messages reflected and reinforced in the fields, woods, and streams and in the trustworthy care of family and of community.

It was a rich and nourishing spiritual life. The snowfalls were pristine and magical and the swamps teemed with life. The church celebrated a "wonder-filled" response to this richness. The love of my parents was unconditional and the reliable backup care of teachers, neighbors, and friends was unfailing. The church taught a message of an infinitely loving, forgiving God and my experience affirmed that indeed the universe was loving and caring.

A highlight of the church year was the annual Easter Walk through which a deep religious teaching of this congregation was conveyed. Each year on the day before Easter the minister and a handful of church-school teachers guided the children on a simple walk into the woods to witness the message that life is truly born from death, that hope springs eternal. In some years, I remember, Easter Saturday was sunny and balmy, but in other years the day was cold and drizzly. Sometimes there were still inches of old snow on the ground and ice still covering the pools and puddles, but without fail we would find new, tender, green shoots under the layers of decaying leaves—life nourished by death. We would always find pollywogs in the waters, even when we had to break through ice. And without fail, the adult companions on this walk were patient, gentle teachers.

Of course, there were hornets and snakes as well as butterflies in the village. There were bullies and shadows and polio and scarlet fever. There was treacherous ice on which my mother fell and for a short time lay bleeding and unconscious, and for the first time I knew that my parents were not invulnerable and that I could not be certain they would always be there for me. I was shaken for a time, but at some deeper level felt assurance that there was a larger net of safety and care that would cradle me.

Today I am co-minister with my husband in a congregation of 150 families in a town of 14,000 people. Members of my congregation come from a dozen or more surrounding towns. Many of them see one another and the church only one morning a week at best. The children come from dozens of different schools, and for many of them attendance at church is sporadic due to the complexities of modern life.

For both parents and children the pace of life is frantic and for too many families there seems to be no unifying focus. The bombardment of information and stimuli is intense, carrying messages that are political, social, and spiritual. Far too many of those messages convey values of materialism and manipulation and prompt feelings of greed, fear, mistrust, and alienation. This is not a centered, secure, coherent village life, but against all odds good parents are working to fashion coherence and meaning.

I would wish for every child the kind of secure and whole childhood with which I was blessed. What was rare even then, in the 1940s and 1950s, is even rarer as we now face the end of the century. I acknowledge this, but I do not relinquish the hope that children and families, even in our fast-paced, segmented, secularized culture, might still have a rich and sustaining experience of religious community at the center of their lives.

Such a grounding religious experience cannot be as easily or naturally available as it was for me. It will require intentionality and commitment on the part of parents and other supportive adults. Such commitment may grow stronger as we gain a greater sense of clarity, understanding what is at stake, what stumbling blocks will be strewn on the path, and what rewards are there, if only the commitment can hold firm.

It is to this end that I offer this book.

The
Sacred

~

When I was a child, the adult church service and children's Sunday school were held at the same hour in our little community church. As the adult service was about to begin, the children were shooed upstairs for their classes so that there would be quiet in the hall just beyond the sanctuary, but I would often linger in that hall to witness the opening ritual.

The organ would conclude the prelude. Then from the back of the sanctuary the minister would proclaim, "God is in his holy temple. Let all the earth keep silence before him." And for a moment there would indeed be silence, a hush that felt to me to be full of a holy presence—just for a moment. Then the minister and choir would offer some phrases in litany, the processional hymn would begin, and I would hurry to join my friends upstairs.

Someone once said, "We are not human beings having a spiritual experience, but spiritual beings having a human experience." What a rare and challenging notion that is! When I first encountered it, it seemed that the very ground shifted beneath me.

The questions in this small book have to do with how we experience the balance of the human and the spiritual in our lives. Where and how do we encounter the holy? Where and how do our children feel its call, its majesty, its strength? To what extent do we, and our children, know ourselves to be spiritual beings? This book is written out of concern that, for most of us, the human side of the scales prevails in such a way that we are diminished. Even as we are surrounded in our living by incredible heights and breadths of thought and experience, art and science, we are impoverished if we lose touch with the holy within and around us.

Before we discuss matters of our children's faith, our children's religious lives, let us look at just what is meant when we talk of these things—the spiritual, the holy, the religious. Let us acknowledge just how elusive these become when we try to capture them in words. Let us begin by reflecting not on definitions of the religious but on the more concrete phenomena of religious spaces and places. These, at least, are tangible, and easy to name and envision. Places of worship can be touched and smelled. They will not slip away as we approach them. They can be visited. Perhaps they can even hold the holy.

Every city, town, and village around the world has particular spots set aside as sacred spaces for the housing of spirits. From grand cathedrals and temples to simple bare meeting houses to sacred groves, places have been designated as holy. I think of the mammoth stone patterns of Stonehenge and Avebury, whose origins and meanings still are not fully understood, and I think of tiny home altars with pictures, flowers, and incense.

Sacred space, whether through intention, history, artistry, or common agreement, can hold a spiritual power. Some spaces may be fresh and personal for us. Other places have deepened in spirituality over time as generations of worshipers wore away the stone steps, generations of dancers deepened the circles in the grove, generations of mourners dampened the air with their tears. Human history can heighten the sense of the sacred. Artistry of design and color can heighten the sense of spirit.

Sacred spaces may be public and communal, or they may be intensely private—a particular tree, cliff, or swamp or a rocking chair by the fireplace where one goes to center, to find strength and meaning, to pray, to cry, or to heal. These places bring clarity, peace, and hope to our lives. The important thing is the power of place to deepen our connection with the holy.

There are potent rituals for creating sacred space—casting circles, lighting candles, invoking spirits with chant, gong, or chime—making space sacred through human call and will. Perhaps in part the power of these rituals lies in the calling of our own awareness into being, calling the spirit within us to presence, to our consciousness. When we create sacred space, we bring with us an attitude of expectancy which in and of itself has some power to generate a response or a reality, to bring into being a living, dancing, spiritual pulse. To invoke is not just to call, but also to quicken, to give life to.

In our long human history our forebears in all ages and places have marked not only holy places, but also holy times—rhythms of the seasons, of the human life cycle, and of dark and light. In every culture and every faith certain times have been marked as holy times, times of poetry rather than prose, times cast with a vibrancy, an extra dimension of life and of energy. Feasts and festivals and holy days have arisen from different sources and have taken different forms, but they have been universal.

This is another way of creating accessibility to divinity, to a sharing in spirituality, through the recognition of and participation in sacred times, times when one opens oneself to the cosmic forces. It is possible for such times to be shaped by an individual, to be personal, intimate, and powerful in that private way, but there is a particular power in those times when the holy is invited and experienced in community. The awareness that others, kindred spirits, are simultaneously opening their hearts and spirits to the sacred can create a profound energy that can deepen the moment and heighten the sense of spiritual connection to others as well as to the transcendent.

Muslims who bow in prayer five times daily know and can feel not only the power of the hundreds of thousands of others bowing at precisely that moment, but also the power of centuries of Muslims who bowed in precisely the same way at precisely the same hours of the day. The sacredness of those moments has been created and re-created to a focused spiritual intensity. When the muezzin announces the prayer from the minaret, profane time is suspended and the Muslim becomes one with sacredness.

In the Jewish tradition, the celebration of the Sabbath is a heightened time of holiness. All holiness is not confined to that one day of the week, but that one day is set aside to lift up, notice, and celebrate all that is holy so that the sense of sacredness will be renewed and refreshed and can be carried forth into the remainder of the week. Although not of the Jewish faith myself, I have been particularly moved by both the philosophy and the practice of Sabbath as I have encountered them in that tradition. I would like to linger just a little on this way of knowing the holy.

The Sabbath, in Jewish tradition, is to be understood as a respite from the daily and the secular, a time not to be productive, but simply to be. It is a time to enjoy family, children, music, good food, and beauty. It is a time to pray and to contemplate, to be renewed. The intent of the Sabbath is not to suggest that the six days of work are negative or unpleasant. In the Torah God commanded that six days were for work just as clearly as he commanded that one day was for rest. The Sabbath is not meant to contrast with the rest of the week, but to be a time to clarify one's priorities, to give stability and focus to the rest of the week, to convey holiness to all of life.

I have had more than one opportunity to share in a Friday evening Sabbath dinner and then to attend synagogue with a Jewish family who honored many of the practices of traditional Sabbath observance. The cooking was completed before sundown, and only the most minimal of serving and clearing was done so full attention could be paid to the beauty of the candles, the table, the ritual, and especially one another. Money cannot be handled on the Sabbath, so in this home where there were young children, payment had already been left on the kitchen table for the babysitter. Cars should not be used on the Sabbath, so we would always walk the half mile to the synagogue. Through these gestures this time, this Friday evening time, became different, special, a time of thoughtfulness about each act performed or refrained from, a time of special care and attention and participation.

The Sabbath is protected by negative rules. One must not work, one must not pursue mundane concerns. But the Sabbath is also adorned with less concrete, but affirmative laws. One must rest and one must rejoice. One must, if one is married, make love with one's mate. It is these affirmations that elicit the sense of the holy. The prohibitions of Sabbath law are intended to free one from the cares and concerns of secularity in order to delight in the beautiful, the spiritual. How liberating not to have to worry about having the right change for the babysitter, or enough gas in the car, or enough milk for breakfast. One is certain to take care of all such mundane details ahead of time if one takes the Sabbath seriously, and so one is free to delight in poetry, in the sharing of thoughts and feelings with family and friends.

Most of us will never observe a time of Sabbath with the kind of discipline intended in this tradition, nor will we find it possible to set aside a stretch of twenty-four hours each week to attend to our spiritual lives. Perhaps, however, we can take to heart the message of the Sabbath that, by deliberately setting aside a time and/or place in which to know, to celebrate, and to honor the holy, we can thereby reclaim our sense of sacredness and carry it into all the days of the week, all the places and activities of our oh-so-secular lives.

The gremlins of time management may be muttering in your ear, scoffing not only at the idea of twenty-four hours each week, but even of two or three hours each week set aside for worship, spiritual nurture, or religious community. Talk back to those gremlins. Talk to them of values and priorities and then tell them about the teachers who insist that the most time-saving thing they do with their classes each day is to take fifteen or twenty minutes at the beginning of the morning to engage the children in meditation or centering exercises. They say that such an investment of time results in the children being more peaceful, more focused, more able to concentrate, cooperate, and learn. And tell them of the minister who says that he prays every morning for one hour. If he has an unusually busy day ahead of him, he prays for two hours.

We may deepen our connection with the sacred by hallowing particular times and places. We may work at simplifying our days. Spirituality, above all else, needs time and space. It needs leisure and breathing room. Unstructured time is the way we define leisure today. We need this, but we also need an attitude of leisure in our structured time, an openness to pause, to linger, to interrupt, to attend to whatever spiritual opportunities may emerge. I have a book whose title conveys the core of its message: *Teacher, the Geranium on the Window Sill Died, and You Just Kept on Talking.* We need an attitude that permits us to heed the plant that died, the seed that sprouted, the fragrance of the night, the cloud that turns a miraculous shade of amethyst, the man who cries, or the fingers that tremble.

Spirituality needs time, and it needs quiet—to focus the attention; to hear the bird that sings, the wind in the grass, the tone of sorrow in the child's voice, the stories of memory; to hear and feel more fully the impulses of one's own heart. Our children are so privileged with opportunities and enrichment, activities that stretch their minds and bodies, develop talents and social skills—all good things, but sometimes too many good things. They, and we, are saturated with stimulation, and it is the loudest, most insistent stimuli that claim our attention. The spiritual calls more often in quiet tones and cannot be heard above the din.

In the Christmas season my colleague Roger A. Cowan wrote:

> "She brought forth her first-born son, wrapped him in swaddling clothes, and laid him in a manger, for there was no room for them in the Inn." That inn has become the most famous of all inns . . . not because of what happened there but because of what MIGHT have happened there and didn't. So it has become a kind of symbol, a parable of your life and mine. Why is so much of life like Bethlehem's inn? Why does so much of love and goodness in our world, of hope and possibility, get shut out? The most obvious reason is that the inn was already full. Those who arrived first were served first. The innkeeper wasn't mean-spirited. Others got there first, the place was full, and that was that.

There is little space or time in our culture to accommodate the holy. Like the inn, the days are filled and that is that.

In the hour of worship in my congregation, people often find tears welling in their eyes and moistening their cheeks. Sniffs and tissues are a part of the ambience as surely as the candles, the stained glass windows, and the smell of coffee. A few folks have told me that they cry in church nearly every Sunday, and I know that this is true not just in my congregation but in others as well. It is my thesis that we cry when we are most touched by the holy.

Some themes, of course, elicit more tears than others. Talking of loss and grief, of healing, of remembrance, and of forgiveness may tap the well of tears more directly, but it may not be the spoken word at all that brings the prickle of crying to eyes and nose, the tremble to the lips. It may be the music; evocations of feeling from old, familiar anthems or hymns; or simply strains of great beauty, tenderness, or glory. It may be a shaft of light or a recognition of tradition that brings the tears. It may be a feeling of safety, trust, and support in a familiar and intimate gathered community, a feeling of acceptance, of embrace.

Most likely, however, it is the readiness of the individual to be touched, to feel deeply, to feel a sense of connection with others and with the movement of the spirit. In that time of worship, of pause, of stillness, we sit at rest and breathe deeply. We turn our minds and hearts to those things that matter most, and we open to a state of wholeness, trust, and receptivity that allows the soul to know and be known, to sing and to dance, to cry.

Sacred time and place can confer this gift, can help to swing open the doors of the heart and the spirit. Sacred time and place can create a sense of safety that allows vulnerability, the falling away of defenses and pretenses to a depth of authenticity that is not possible to sustain through most of the hours and days of our lives.

It is the life-giving premise of this book that there is a sacredness in our world and in our human condition, that there is a holy, mysterious power and presence within and among us. This holiness may be known in moments of exquisitely tender love or deep meditation. It may be glimpsed in sunrise through the mist, felt as the down on a newborn's head, and heard in the song of birds at dusk. It may be manifested in the brilliance of new vision or selfless, sacrificial giving. It may take the form of strength arising out of anguish or true dedication arising out of moral failure.

We are more than flesh and blood. Our potential is for more than material success. There is healing that medical experts cannot explain. There is hope when there is no reason to hope. Our earth is more than soil and water. Our sky, ravaged as it has been, continues to hold magic and mystery.

It is also the life-giving premise of this book that, to the extent that we can become aware of, in touch with, guided by this center of sacredness, our individual lives will become richer, fuller, and more whole and thus will become more holy. We will become both more fully human and more fully divine. As we are more in touch with this spiritual core of ourselves and of the universe, we will live more intensely, more joyfully, more peacefully, and with a greater sense of harmony with and connectedness to all of life and to the source of life. To the extent that we are aware of and live through this center of sacredness that is common to all humanity, even to all of life, we will be participating in a common life rather than our individual lives. We will be acting to enrich the life of all humanity and will assume our measure of responsibility for all of life.

The more fully we know the holy, the clearer and more grounded we will be. Confusions and irrelevancies will fall away. Our energies will be more focused and we will be able to be more creative and more productive. Our hearts will open wider and we will be able to be more generous and more compassionate. The reality of our connectedness to one another and to all of life will be felt more deeply, and we will be moved to more responsible living.

The more fully we know the holy, the more we will be healed of old angers and hatreds and be able to forgive those who have hurt us. The more fully we know the holy, the richer and more fulfilling our own lives will be, and the more we will give to the people and the world around us to deepen and enrich their lives as well.

This sacredness, by its very nature, is elusive, impossible to name and to describe, and we may be glad that it is so. If it could be captured and boxed, it would lose its majesty. Although we will never abandon our continual use of words to point toward this elusive wonder, to capture crumbs and fragments of it, we know the holy is to be felt and lived rather than described. It may be felt in prayer, in love, in service to others. It may be felt in particular moments in the natural world, in personal moments of creative energy, in chaos, and in order. It may be felt in the passage of birth and in the passage from life into death.

The holy is present always and available to us always. Each moment holds beauty, texture, history, connection, and possibility, but we know and feel only a fraction, and in most moments we bypass the spiritual entirely. Perhaps we could not bear such richness. Like Emily in Thornton Wilder's *Our Town,* we would say, "Oh, earth, you're too wonderful for anybody to realize you. Do any human beings ever realize life while they live it?—every, every minute?"

The attitude of mindfulness, made so accessible to us in recent years particularly by the work of Thich Nhat Hahn, guides us gently in the direction of this fuller connection with the spiritual in every moment of our lives, living fully with each breath, each step, each dish we wash, knowing fully the richness and beauty of each moment. It is a glorious discipline, and we need disciplines, practices, and ways to nurture our connection with the sacred.

We need disciplines to help us to move toward mindfulness in every moment. We also need the discipline of setting aside a time each week to renew and reconnect with the spirit.

The
Culture

~

When I was a child there wasn't much on Sunday mornings to keep us from going to church. There were no soccer games, no malls, no television programming. There was a Sunday paper, thick with comics. There were cows to be milked and, for the moms, a Sunday dinner to prepare, but not much else laid claim on the day. Except for these minimal tasks, work came to a halt. Entertainment and recreation were largely home-grown affairs, so there was no external pull away from family and community.

It was easy to go to church. There was nothing to deter one except sloth. It was what most people did on Sunday mornings. There was even a certain peer pressure to go to church, or at least to send your children to Sunday school.

There was a time, in many ways a simpler time, when weekends were free of distractions and demands, and going to church or temple was easier than it is today. Contemporary patterns of work and "structured" leisure have taken over weekends. Once it was only hospital workers who worked on Saturdays and Sundays, with doctors, firefighters, and emergency workers on call as needed. Now retail sales operate seven days a week, long hours each day. The vast food and entertainment industry peaks on Saturdays and Sundays. Business people who travel more and more frequently for conferences, trade shows, or business meetings often have to travel over the weekend. Flex time and telecommuting have their advantages, but also mitigate against clear, predictable schedules that block out time for leisure just as surely as time for work.

Some employers are so insensitive to the religious lives of their employees that workers have to sue for the right to be free on their days of religious observance. How many others whose religious lives are complicated by their work commitments might wish to participate in their particular religious community but lack the energy, the clarity, or the resources to act on this wish?

The mobility of our generation has pulled families and long-time friends hundreds and thousands of miles apart. Weekends are often the only time to visit grandparents or college roommates. Children's social lives, which once were spontaneous, organic neighborhood happenings, are increasingly scheduled and arranged, with little if any thought given to the possible importance of family attendance at church or synagogue. Birthday parties and other celebrations often are Friday or Saturday night sleepovers, and the sports team phenomenon is an unleashed monster devouring all kinds of family life, including times of family worship.

There is no shared cultural time to be still, no common time when families can easily be together. In this latter part of the twentieth century there is no communal experience of Sabbath, as a Saturday or Sunday visit to any shopping mall will attest. And there is little peer support for arranging a weekly schedule in which churchgoing is assumed. To attempt to create within a single family such an abiding commitment is a mountainous challenge.

Our lives are so very, very busy. For too many of us, religion has become marginalized in our thinking and our valuing, and thus in our daytimers as well. Religious community has come to be viewed as an optional kind of "add-on," to be dabbled in when it is convenient, to be put on the list of resolutions in seasons of new beginning—September, January—like intentions to diet and to keep one's desk free of clutter. It is to be fit into one's weekend if there isn't too much else going on: if there are no house guests or sports playoffs, if the laundry and the bills are caught up, if the leaves are raked and the garden is in, and if the surf's not up and the ski season hasn't started yet.

Within our larger society, to be sure, there are subcultures in which churchgoing is assumed. There are groups in which it is expected that both adults and children will participate in church life and in which social and other events are scheduled accordingly. In such groups there is a broad-based, positive attitude toward churchgoing, valuing the power of worship, prayer, and religious community. If one's personal inclination does not lure one to church or temple, it's almost irrelevant. One simply goes to church. That is the way it is, and the life of the community shapes itself to accommodate the church's schedule.

There are such subcultures, but they are not the norm. In most neighborhoods, families have to make determined commitments and buck prevailing forces and trends to ensure that religious community is a central and centering dimension of their lives.

The schedules and the lifestyles of our communities are great seducers and shapers, but there are deeper, even more subtle forces at work as well. *Boston Globe* columnist Ellen Goodman writes of the constant battle parents must wage with our culture today.

Mothers and fathers are expected to screen virtually every aspect of their children's lives. To check the ratings on the movies; to read the labels on the CDs, to find out if there's MTV in the house next door. . . . It isn't that (parents) can't say no, but that there's so much more to say no to. . . . [We] once expected parents to raise their children in accordance with the dominant cultural messages. Today they are expected to raise them in opposition [to the culture].

And nowhere is this more true than in the matter of spiritual nurture. The howls of materialism, alienation, speed, and greed are deafening. We are a profoundly secular culture. Publicly, collectively, we honor technology and human achievement. We invest in material goods and value the dollar above all else. We nod politely to the spiritual, but do not really allow any room for the transcendent to be weighed seriously in our shared journey of life, liberty, and the pursuit of happiness.

In his book *The Culture of Disbelief*, Stephen Carter has captured this reality in a compelling way, describing how the rhetoric of our society trivializes religious faith. He cites example after example of how relentlessly, day after day, journalists, politicians, educators, and public spokespersons of all kinds erode the value of religion in small and subtle ways, juxtaposing it to the weighty values of science, reason, and, above all, success.

> The consistent message of modern American society is that whenever the demands of one's religion conflict with what one has to do to get ahead, one is expected to ignore the religious demands and act . . . well . . . *rationally.* (p. 13)

The commercial nature of some of the recent spiritual movements is another manifestation of the trivializing of religion. In this arena, faith is isolated from community and tradition, then packaged and sold for $29.95. Spiritual truth is offered in six easy lessons and spirituality is distorted into a variation of self-help programs. Although there may be value in these programs, to consider them as a meaningful alternative to a community of faith and tradition is a very sad reflection of the way religious community is perceived. The highly visible nature of these spiritual quick fixes is a layer of glitz on our cultural images of religion, a diminishing and trivializing gloss, a mockery and an insult to deep faith.

Culturally we may pay some lip service to the values of spirituality, but consider the extent to which those values are really granted any honor or power. Consider the powers to which we turn for healing. We know that spiritual well-being, hope, faith, and inner peace all contribute to physical well-being. It has been well documented that people who are devout, who are clear in their faith, who are meaningfully connected to religious communities, and who are actively engaged in prayer or meditation recover more quickly and fully from serious illnesses and injuries. We know that the surest way to health is through a blend of medical, social, and spiritual attention. As a society we know this to be true, yet how do we evidence our honoring of this knowledge?

There have been many cases over the years in which parents who are Christian Scientists or Seventh Day Adventists have been challenged for neglecting to secure medical attention for their children. Parents have been sued, penalized, vilified, and even imprisoned for placing all their hopes for healing in prayer and faith. Without either condoning or condemning this aspect of these faiths, I simply ask you to reflect on the fact that the reverse never, ever occurs. It simply never happens that parents who secure adequate medical attention for their children are publicly challenged or criticized or brought before the courts of law for withholding from those children the healing powers of faith, prayer, or religious community.

It strains the limits of imagination to conjure up such a scenario. Try, if you will, to imagine that parents who take their children for regular checkups, see that they are up to date on their inoculations, consult a doctor if fever persists or injury occurs, but fail to give these children a grounding in religious faith might be called to account if a child were to fall gravely or even terminally ill. Imagine a lawsuit against parents who fail to pray with or for their children, who fail to feed their spirits as well as their bodies.

These same parents, who care so attentively for their children's physical being, care equally for their secular education, making every effort to see that they attend school regularly and do their homework responsibly. Conscientious parents oversee these homework assignments, support the children's search for resources, meet with teachers, track the grades, never questioning the value of this dimension of their children's growth and development. But many of these conscientious parents fail to give similar attention to the religious and spiritual development of their sons and daughters.

It is my conviction that these parents value a grounding in faith for their children as highly as they value a grounding in literacy, but that they are unclear about how such faith might be nurtured. They underestimate the importance of intentional guidance and culturally there are few reminders or supports for them. I believe that most parents value the power of moral and ethical development as highly as they value math skills, but perhaps they do not see that these religious dimensions of their children's development need a structure and a community to guide them just as their secular education does. This is particularly true in a climate where many of the loudest voices are calling from self-interest rather than from a valuing of the common good.

Although parents may want their children to become strong, mature people of faith, they may not know where to turn for the support and structure they need. Churches and synagogues must bear some responsibility for this. Too often they have offered religious training that was outdated, irrelevant to daily life, poorly designed and/or taught, and sometimes even damaging to the emotional well-being of the children in their care. Too often they still do. Many parents carry this image of formal religious education, either from stories they have heard or from their own experiences. It sometimes seems a well-kept secret that there are other kinds of religious education available—vital, relevant, and engaging religious education opportunities—and so parents never even embark on the hard work of seeking these out.

As if all this weren't enough for parents to face in the desire to support their children's religious growth and development, there is yet another dimension to this struggle, and that is the children's own resistance. A few years ago a Doonesbury comic strip by Gary Trudeau featured Mike and J. J. posing the idea of going to church to their daughter Alex. Her response predictably is, "Church? Church is boring! . . . Didn't you think church was boring when you were a kid?" And Mike says, "Well, sure, I hated going, but church was good for me, so my parents made me stick it out. You may end up hating church, too, but you have to come by that feeling honestly. You have to put in the pew time, like Mom and I did."

"Oh," says Alex. "What if I like it?" And the parents respond in befuddled amusement, "Like it? What do you mean?"

As he does so often, Trudeau captures an essential contemporary human reality in this comic strip. In popular thought and imagery, participation in a religious community may be viewed as something good for you like broccoli and daily flossing, but not as a slice of life that might be enjoyed, even eagerly anticipated, and certainly not as an organic, integrated strand of one's basic living, as essential as air, water, and human relationships. This is an image held by many parents and, unfortunately, held by many children once they reach a certain age.

When they are very young, children may be delighted to go to church or temple with their families—if those religious communities are welcoming and happy places for children, and if they go regularly enough that the place of worship feels familiar and secure to them. But all too soon comes the day when it is not the culture but your own child pulling back from churchgoing. In my community this tends to happen at about fourth or fifth grade, but I expect there may be variations in the timing from one community to another.

There are several sources for this resistance, and it is important to understand them and not simply take at face value the child's complaints that he or she finds church school stupid and boring. These preadolescent children are at a stage where much of what they learn is through testing. They are testing, among other things, their parents' priorities, finding out what they really believe in and what they merely bow to politely, and they are testing how much control they can have over their own lives.

Like an animal that can smell the weakness of its prey, children sense their parents' ambivalence or tentativeness in their commitment to church, and there they plant their flag of rebellion. They need to win some ground, some domain of control. They know they won't win a struggle against homework or the dentist, but church is another matter, and when parents yield to a child's plea to stay home from church or synagogue, they are saying that religion really isn't all that important.

This may be the age at which the cultural message of "church is for sissies" begins to be felt. Historically, church life has revolved around women (except for its professional leadership), casting an aura of sentimentality around it, an aura that spills over into an image of church as wimpy and childish, and the preadolescent who is cherishing a more grown up image feels yet another tug away. When this image is juxtaposed with the pulls of the sports teams and other more socially prestigious activities, the church hardly stands a chance.

This also is the time when the first urges to break away from the family begin to surface. The urge to separate from family is a complex one. In part, it is a need to break away in terms of public association, to be seen as one of the gang, not as child with parents. Growing children also have a deeper psychic need to stand alone and apart, to create their own life and community, to shape and define their own values, to become autonomous beings. These inner needs for authentic autonomy, developmentalists tell us, are inescapable, and the resulting struggles between parents and teens have been with us for generations. The need for an autonomous identity is real, natural, and healthy. It is the appropriate work of the teen years to challenge and to separate.

The outer manifestations of this natural developmental phase, however, have taken on a life of their own. It has become a kind of cultural persona emerging at younger and younger ages as our children are prodded into growing up, or at least appearing to grow up, faster and faster. Thus, as young as nine and ten, it becomes unfashionable to go places with mom and dad, to do things as a family. And even the most committed, faithful of families will find their preadolescent children resisting the call to church on Sunday morning, to synagogue on Friday evening.

Many parents yield to their children's resistance. "They are so busy six days of the week," they say. "They need one day to sleep late, to have unstructured time, to relax." I wouldn't quarrel for a moment with this parental concern for the crowding of their children's lives, but I would question the assumption that church should be the first to go. I would ask parents to look closely at their priorities and to be deliberate in weighing and choosing what is to fill their days and their children's days. I would ask that they claim for themselves their rightful responsibility to determine how precious time will be used, and not to let unreflected cultural pressures shape their family's values. Is it really religious community that should be relinquished first, when life becomes too full? What would happen if participation in church or temple was held as a nonnegotiable priority and not even considered as an option in easing the pace of life?

"I was forced to go to church as a child," many parents say. "I hated it and quit as soon as I was given the choice. I don't want my child to learn to hate church as I did." I have two responses to this common claim. First, not all church or synagogue experiences are alike. If your child-hood experience really was deadly dull, or if it gnawed away at your self-esteem or filled you with fear and anger, or in some other way appropriately evoked your hatred, of course you don't want to inflict a comparable experience on your child, and you shouldn't. It is your job to find an engaging, substantive, life-affirming religious education program so you can be sure that, if your child complains, it isn't because the program is perni-cious, but for some other reason. Don't assume that your child's resistance is comparable to the hatred you felt.

Second, and perhaps more important, the dynamic through which you engage your child in religious com-munity need not be felt as force. A gentle insistence, an uncompromising expectation coming from your own deep valuing of the experience, need not be felt as force. With thought and care, with strong modeling, with clar-ity of commitment and a carefully chosen religious community, parents can minimize the struggle and bitterness surrounding this issue.

Children, of course, resist all kinds of things in life that their parents nevertheless insist on: appropriate bedtimes, green vegetables, thank you notes, book reports. Why should the matter of attendance at church or synagogue be treated any differently?

My two sons, now grown, may have had even more reason to resist churchgoing than their peers, since they had not just one, but two parents who were ministers. If any children ever needed to rebel against their religious community, mine did. My husband and I were clear and firm in our expectations, however, and their resistance was minimal. It was simply understood that through the eighth grade they would participate in the church school every Sunday, unless they were ill. Only once or twice a year was there any other event so compelling that we would even contemplate making an exception. Church was the priority.

Of course they grumbled a bit, but because we were firm and consistent the grumbling never grew to a roar. Because we were familiar with the church school program and convinced of its value, because we knew that it was relevant, age-appropriate, and creative in engaging the children's interest, we gave little credence to their pro forma complaints. The test came when they completed eighth grade and were then free to choose for themselves their level of church participation. Each, when his time came, chose to attend the high school youth group with a passion.

Because they had bonded with the church community, become close friends with their church peers, felt comfortable and cared for there, their connection to the religious community remained strong and vital. Because they had found their experiences at church to have some value (maybe not every time, but often enough), they wanted to continue to participate. Perhaps most importantly, because there was no question about the value their parents placed on this experience, at some deep level they trusted that there was value there for them as well.

These are the mountains to be climbed: a secular culture that trivializes religion and fills seven days a week with busyness, leaving no room for the spirit; an image of religion as wimpish and irrelevant to real life; children who will resist our efforts to ground them in faith. The concerned parent must be well fortified with canteens filled with clarity of purpose and stout shoes of determination.

Rabbi Moshe Waldoks worries about the parents who take their children to sports games on Saturday mornings, the Jewish sabbath, instead of to synagogue. He says:

> I often go out to groups and say, "How many want your kids to be professional soccer players?" Of course, nobody raises their hand. . . . Then I say, "How many want them to be Jews at the end of the century?" Oh! Everyone raises

their hand. So where's the investment? You're investing in soccer and you want your kids to be Jews? Something is wrong. (*Boston Globe,* October 22, 1996)

How many of you want your children to become adults secure in and enlivened by their faith? How will you support them in that direction?

The
Children

~

When I was a child, the fields and forest were my playground as they have been for generations of children and still are for a lucky few. I can remember moments of lying in a meadow, grass and wild flowers tall above me, vast sky overhead, insects buzzing and brushing by me. In such moments I felt a sense of near dissolution into the earth, the sky, the grasses, moments of feeling that the boundary between me and the meadow was a permeable boundary, not clearly defined by the layer of skin on my body, but a gentle merging of me into it, it into me. When I was child I was a spiritual being—as all children are spiritual beings.

Whether we wish it so or not, our children are religious, spiritual beings. From within their own magical selves they know feelings, intuitions, and impulses. From the people, stories, songs, and media of their environs they hear religious words and messages and see religious symbols and images. From the experiences of their daily living they encounter religious events. They see dry sticks sprout pulsing green leaves. They see the deer killed on the highway. They watch their teacher's tummy grow round with new life, and bid farewell to their uncle dying of AIDS. From the demands of their living and growing in the world they face situations that require from them a religious decision, response, or interpretation. We cannot choose whether they will be religious, but we can choose how and to what extent we will support, guide, and celebrate this dimension of their nature.

Children are deeply religious beings on every level. Intellectually they think and conceptualize on matters of good and evil, of God and prayer, of life and death. Emotionally they feel deep compassion and empathy, as well as unbounded hope and deep despair. Spiritually they enjoy a sense of awe and wonder that far exceeds our adult possibilities; they have insights of transcendence, even mystical experiences. Behaviorally they live out kindness and cruelty, generosity and selfishness, for-giveness and condemnation. And physically, sensually (and I submit that the spiritual is, in part, a deeply sensual matter), they are blessed with extraordinary gifts.

Edward Robinson, a generation ago, did some interesting research from his institute at Manchester College, Oxford, England, into the spiritual, mystical experiences of children. His work unfolded through interviews with adults about their memories of the religious from their childhood years. His work *The Original Vision* yields some fascinating material, as adult after adult reports memories of powerful, vivid, transformative experiences in her or his childhood. This is an example of the kind of life-changing experience recalled.

My mother and I were walking on a stretch of land in Pangbourne Berks, known locally as "the moors." As the sun declined and the slight chill of evening came on, a pearly mist formed over the ground. My feet, with the favourite black shoes with silver buckles, were gradually hidden from sight until I stood ankle deep in gently swirling vapour. Here and there just the very tallest harebells appeared above the mist. I had a great love of these exquisitely formed flowers, and stood lost in wonder at the sight.

Suddenly I seemed to see the mist as a shimmering gossamer tissue and the harebells, appearing here and there, seemed to shine with a brilliant fire. Somehow I understood that this was the living tissue of life itself, in which that which we call consciousness was embedded, appearing here and there as a shining focus of energy in the more diffused whole. In that moment I knew that I had my own special place, as had all other things, animate and so-called inanimate, and that we were all part of this universal tissue which was both fragile yet immensely strong, and utterly good and beneficent. (p. 32)

More recent work by Lorelie J. Farmer of Gordon College in Massachusetts has affirmed Robinson's findings. Both Robinson and Farmer found that children have insights and experiences that leave them with a remarkable sense of certainty regarding human nature, morality, and spiritual or religious reality. This knowledge was unrelated to and often inconsistent with what they were taught at home or in church and left lasting influences that subsequently shaped their lives.

Reading these narratives brought to my own consciousness comparable memories—memories of childhood times when I felt an almost mystical oneness with an ongoing stream of life. Other adults with whom I have shared both Robinson's research and my own memories have affirmed that they too had such experiences. Are such experiences, we might wonder, reflective of some central truth more readily accessible to children than to adults whose years and layers of living have tarnished their spiritual knowing?

Some philosophies of child development and education have conceived of children as having a clearer and truer understanding of the holy than adults. The Transcendentalists of the early nineteenth century in New England felt that infants, having just arrived from the hand of God, were closer to divinity. They saw this as a time of ultimate wisdom, a kind of spiritual knowing that would become cluttered and confused and faded as the children grew and encountered layers of conflicting ideas. The purpose of education in this school of thought is not to impart new knowledge, for the most important knowledge is already within. The purpose of education is to guide the child's behavior into harmony with the truths the child already knows, encouraging the innate urge toward goodness and kindness.

Although I would not go quite as far as these Transcendentalist thinkers in attributing innate religious knowledge to children, my own childhood experiences and my experiences with children in my congregation over the years lead me to believe that children do have an inner sense of the holy quite apart from any messages they receive from the people around them.

We are accustomed to hearing quaint, charming, and sometimes enigmatic things from children. The younger the child, the odder the thoughts or images might seem, and we chuckle and tell these cute stories to our friends. But perhaps sometimes there may be meaningful spiritual insight or sensation lying behind these cute phrases. Perhaps children try to tell us more than we are ready to hear, and they quickly learn to keep to themselves some of their tenderest or most vibrant feelings and knowings because they are not taken seriously. Perhaps we fear that which children know because we sense that it holds such mystery and power.

Simply finding adequate words to describe and express the spiritual is impossible even for adults. In their innocence young children may try to communicate, but if they are not heard and honored, will soon begin to guard these feelings against the laughter of the world.

I never told anyone about my "meadow moments." Somehow I had learned that such things were not to be talked about. But perhaps if I could have shared them with others, they would have felt more real and I might have drawn greater strength and meaning from them. If we could truly hear our children, we might empower them to own and draw more deeply upon their insights, thus becoming more conscious of themselves as spiritual beings. If we could truly hear our children, we might learn a great deal. We might learn how to free our own memories and to reconnect with a kind of spiritual openness.

Looking at children's spiritual and religious lives from a different perspective, David Heller has explored children's ideas and images of God and found them to be rich and varied. Heller's work was done with children of families who had a clear and articulated religious faith.

Not surprisingly, the children's images reflected the prevailing ideas of their family's particular tradition.

It should be no surprise that Heller found every child holding an image of God. But even those children who may never have entered a church, synagogue, or mosque and whose parents may not claim any faith at all, even such children have a notion of who or what God is. Every child hears this word GOD nearly daily—in blessing when someone sneezes, in curse in countless other moments; as expletive in tones ranging from awe to disgust; as referent, whether vague or specific, in comic strips and television shows. When a word is so common in both public and private discourse, of course children will form some meaning around it, whether or not anyone ever explicitly discusses with them who or what God may be.

And the child knows, from the varying contexts and from the exaggerated tones, that this is not a casual concept or being. It is a very important one. "Oh, my God!" "God bless you." "God damn it." "God willing." Perhaps you have heard the wonderful story of the young child busily working on a picture. When her father asked what she was drawing, she replied, "A picture of God." "But no one knows what God looks like," said the father. "They will when I'm finished," came the confident response.

Children can know things with such certainty. Unless we are careful and proactive in hearing their thoughts, responding to them and sharing our own, unless we surround them with stories, songs, and other messages that carry positive images of who or what God may be, or may not be, the notions of God they develop may be damaging ones. They may be notions of a monstrous man in the sky watching their every move, ready to pounce and to punish, or a shadowy figure waiting to whisk them away to heaven.

But, parents may ask, how can we teach our children about God when our own ideas are vague and unformed? How and why can we teach our children when we don't believe in God ourselves? Robinson reports the following conversation:

> I remember sitting in my mother's lap at the age of five, while she affectionately explained that the idea of a God was a very nice and poetic way of explaining things, but just like a fairy tale. I felt embarrassed at what seemed abysmal blindness and ignorance and felt sorry for her. (p. 69)

We must take seriously that children think about God and, regardless of the parents' belief or unbelief, for at least some portion of their childhood children will believe in God. They would be well supported by parents and others who are willing to engage in conversation around this, hearing the children's ideas and concerns and welcoming their pictures.

It is helpful for such adults continually to say that there are lots of different ideas about God, that no one knows for sure, that God is too wonderful to be fully known and understood. It is helpful to use a variety of words, names, and descriptive phrases—Holy Spirit, Spirit of Life, God of Love, God of Earth and Sky, Goddess of Earth and Sky, Goddess Within, God Within—to keep the thinking always open-ended. And it is very important that the images and language be embracing and strengthening rather than threatening. A proper discussion of how to talk with a child about God would require a whole book unto itself, and I refer parents wanting to pursue this to Harold Kushner's *When Children Ask About God*, listed in the suggested reading section at the end of the book.

When language fails, and it probably will, sometimes art, movement, or another form of creative expression will help to keep the conversation open and fruitful. Color, symbol, and shape—relationships of colors, symbols, and shapes—sometimes can express ideas and feelings that are limited by language. Music, dance, or the language of poetry rather than prose might capture a vision or a longing that otherwise might slip away.

The topic of God, of course, is the big one, but it is not the only religious word or concept to which your children will be exposed and to which they will attach meanings and beliefs. They will have notions about heaven and hell, and perhaps about the devil. They will hear bits of stories and names of people and places from the Bible. These stories are complex, located in a particular socio-historical context as well as a particular theological framework. They can be told in many ways and subject to many interpretations, and your children deserve some help in understanding what they hear.

They will hear prayers and will hear about prayers and may have an interest in praying if it is not already a part of their life. There are many standard prayers from the various religious traditions, of course, but if these feel unauthentic, you might want to create your own. Parents might set aside some quiet moments at bedtime to reflect with their children on: (1) something from the day for which you each are thankful; (2) something you are sorry for; (3) something you intend for tomorrow.

Children's questions will come, but it has been my experience that children can abide quite comfortably with unanswered questions, with mystery and wonder. They can even revel in the unknown, delight in the wondering. "Twinkle, twinkle, little star. How I wonder what you are!" What matters is that their questions be heard, honored, and responded to. The response may be, probably often should be, "I wonder about that too," or "I think maybe . . . , but I'm not sure."

The important thing is that the child be companioned in his or her religious thinking and encouraged to continue in it. The bigger the circle of people with whom your child can join in this conversation and exploration, the fuller and richer his or her sense of the holy will become. Children are evolving as religious beings, whether we wish it to be so or not. We can choose to be active influences in this evolution, or we can leave the child vulnerable to random messages and meanings from wherever and whomever they may come.

Children *will* feel moments of intense compassion and empathy, of heightened and delightful sensory awareness, of healing and renewal, of creativity, even of magic. This is a given of our human nature. If they are given the gift of a thoughtful religious environment, they will be more likely to pause to savor such moments, to name and nurture them. They will have the capacity to celebrate them more fully and will have language with which to connect them with the spiritual.

Reverend Clinton Lee Scott, a wonderful, wise old minister, now gone, wrote this parable "Of A Foolish Father."

And there was a certain man that had a son whom he greatly loved. And he thought within himself saying, None is wise enough to instruct my son in the mysteries of the eternal: neither priest nor Levite shall tell him what is good and what is evil, lest his mind be corrupted with error. And he saith, This shall he do: he shall wait until he is a man, then he shall know of himself what to believe.

But it was not as the father thought. For the son did grow and was strong. Keepeth he his eyes open for seeing, and his ears for hearing. And his teachers were neither priests nor Levites. Neither did he come to the Temple for instruction. But his teachers were them that speaketh into the air, and them that were seen in the pictures of Babylon, and messengers in bright colors that were brought into the household on the morning of the Sabbath day.

And when the father was old he understood that the mind of his son had not been as an empty vessel that waiteth for a day to be filled, but that it was like unto a parched field that drinketh of that which falleth upon it.

The
Parents

~

When I was a child, nearing the end of childhood, I rode in the back seat with a friend as my mother chauffeured us to or from some junior high school event. My friend and I argued the matter of capital punishment. Criminals should not be killed, I argued, because all people are basically good and would never freely and willingly harm another person. Those who harm others must have been subjected to such inhumane treatment and conditions in their own lives that their criminal acts are simply desperate, aberrant ones. They, therefore, should not be punished but rehabilitated.

I honestly believed that I had developed this philosophy completely on my own and was appalled when my mother said, "You sound just like your father." My passion came from the deep well of religious conviction regarding human nature, a conviction learned from my father and embedded so deeply that it still shapes my life today. I still speak against capital punishment, with more sophistication I like to think, but from the same well of faith in the essential goodness of our human nature.

Parents are, without question, the primary religious educators of their children—and ought to be. This is one of the most profound of parental responsibilities, but sadly, one too often neglected. Just as children's bodies need balanced nutrition, inoculations, and protection from toxins, accidents, and other harm; just as children's minds need challenge and stimulation, training, and basic tools, their souls and spirits also need nurture and guidance.

Tender loving care is a given for most modern parents, as are support and encouragement for creative expression. We do well at coaching in kindness, compassion, generosity, and ethical decision making. These are all pieces, important pieces, of the work of religious or spiritual parenting, but there are other important pieces that are less likely to be lived out intentionally. When the parenting is not intentional, much may be conveyed unintentionally, and there may be alarming omissions. As with sex education, our children do not remain untouched by what parents neglect to teach. As "The Foolish Father" learned, they are then vulnerable to teachings from random and perhaps pernicious sources.

Messages abound, both bold and subtle, from the media and other voices of the culture. Fairy tales, cartoons, and children's literature carry sometimes potent meanings and messages. Teachers' and caregivers' religious or spiritual assumptions permeate their interactions with children. Peer influences are inevitable, varied, often unstable, and increasingly powerful as children grow toward adolescence. All these and more are shapers of a child's religious being, but none of these is as formative as the messages and meanings conveyed by parents.

It is the parents who affirm and reinforce particular religious ideas and discount others. It is the stories told by the parents that are held closest to the heart and the images offered by parents that have the greatest power. It is the language used by parents that becomes familiar and comfortable, with nuances of meaning carried in the tone of voice and the stance of the body. These nuances are conveyed to the child as truth. Parents are the constant presence year after year through every stage of the child's development, every stage of vulnerability, impressionability, and readiness. They are the trusted ones whose values and religious beliefs are imbibed daily along with mother's milk, bedtime stories, comfort when they hurt, and reassurance when they fear.

This parental influence is enormous, but acknowledging this enormity may, and perhaps should, be felt as both relief and distress. It may be heartening to be reassured that our children are not helpless victims of others' religious ideologies, which we may perceive to be dangerous and malformative, damaging both to the child's own being and to the well-being of our communities. It will be welcome news that, at least into the adolescent years and usually into adulthood, children reflect their parents' faith.

The distress may enter when parents realize the awesomeness of this influence and feel unprepared. It is the fortunate but rare parent who feels clear and strong and ready to be the religious educator of his or her children. It is the fortunate but rare parent who had a strong, consistent religious tradition in his or her own childhood, who is still able as an adult to embrace that tradition, and who shares the work of parenting with a partner whose faith is at least consistent with, if not the same as, his or her own.

Many parents of today were not raised in an actively religious tradition. They bring to this dimension of their parenting only a fuzzy, undefined sense of their own personal religion. There may be a sense of something spiritual in their lives. There may be scattered traces of religious teachings, songs, or stories in their memories, but no coherent, grounded, articulated sense of faith.

These adults are likely to have parents (grandparents to the children of today) who *were* active in a particular faith, who *were* engaged in a religious community that nurtured, clarified, and articulated their religious lives. Through ritual and repetition, stories and songs, the grandparents' faith was imaged and reinforced. They knew what they believed and why. They knew where to seek support. In turn, these elders may have passed on to their own children (now parents) a sustaining kind of faith. Without regular participation in communal worship, however, without the years of ritual and teaching, without the benefit of religious community, the faith of those children (now parents) is likely to be ungrounded and inaccessible.

Today's parents may not feel a lack of faith at their own center. This was passed on to them from the certainty in their parents' lives. Now that it is their watch—their turn to pass on this spiritual grounding—the firmness of the faith eludes them. The center doesn't hold. What language they have feels archaic and disconnected. They may know that they are believers but aren't quite sure just what it is they believe. The fullness of the tradition, a fullness of conviction and connection, is not available to them. They may recall fragments of stories, but the message is no longer intact or relevant. There may be bits of theology or ideology in their heads, but without a full context such bits do not cohere. Rituals may still move them and feel essential to their lives, but again without depth of context, such rituals become disconnected and shallow. In this turning of the generations we find that what was held too loosely has now slipped away.

For other parents, their experience may have been of a religious tradition they can no longer embrace. Parents who were raised in a religious tradition but then rejected it because it felt limiting or irrelevant, or perhaps even damaging, will find the role of parent as religious educator to be extremely confusing. If their faith was rejected with anger or hurt, the parents may well project feelings of anger and mistrust toward religious institutions in general.

When two parents come from different religious roots, the struggle to blend, balance, and honor those varying traditions can be daunting. Too often the struggle is abandoned, leaving a vacuum of overt religious celebration but a muddy undercurrent of mixed theological messages. Hurts and resentments arising from the tension of trying to embrace two traditions may permeate whatever religious messages are conveyed to the children.

Sometimes one parent who cares deeply about his or her faith works to transmit this while the other, perhaps unintentionally, undermines that effort, conveying by his or her disinterest a message that religion is unimportant. When parents are separated or divorced, such mixed messages become particularly pronounced and may even be exaggerated in manipulative, divisive ways. Even in intact marriages, however, such messages can deeply confuse the child.

In all of these cases, and in countless variations on these themes, we find parents who are not prepared to nurture their children in a clear and compelling spiritual path. Well intentioned though they may be, there is no deep, unified, and unifying faith within them to hand on to their children.

And so parents should first take seriously their own religious grounding, their own religious education, their own spiritual nurture. Parents should take every opportunity to study, reflect, pray, and clarify their own faith. Study and discussion groups, reading, journal writing, or other creative expressions are all helpful tools. Therapy might even be of value if there are unresolved conflicts or deep hurts in the parents' religious past or if there are deep religious differences between parents.

The most effective way for parents to prepare for their work as religious educators, however, is immersion in a religious community. There they can have the support, structure, and power of gathered worship to help them clarify and establish who they are as religious beings. There they can find help to articulate their faith, first for themselves, and then for their children.

The theologian Langdon Gilkey calls this "languaging the encounter," putting into words the deepest knowing of our souls, the ultimate allegiances of our lives, the sources of strength and healing to be turned to when trouble comes—and trouble does come to everyone. I call parents to religious community not just for help in working through the articulation of their faith (although this alone is the work of a lifetime), but also to be nourished. In religious community their faith may be nourished to grow in clarity and strength and may be conveyed to their children as a robust source of nurture. Deep and sustaining faith is more than a system of belief, more than ideas about religious matters. Faith, felt at the core of one's being, gives meaning and direction to life. It heals and supports. It is a holding, a cushion of care, a certainty of trust.

The centering and strengthening of religious rituals, the release and commitment that come through communal prayer, the joy of shared celebration, working together with like-minded people, and serving as companion, guide, and comforter to one another—all of these dimensions of the experience of religious community help to deepen one's faith.

Erik Erikson, the great psychotherapist who has left us such a legacy of insight into psychosocial development and the interlinking of the generations in this development, said, "Many are proud to be without religion whose children cannot afford their being without it." He was referring to the way that faith, or the lack of faith, is conveyed from parent to child. Parents who have a sense of purpose and belonging, a connection to a source of strength and meaning beyond themselves, and a sense that there is something ultimate on which to rely communicate that deep, unarticulated sense of faith and trust to the child in a thousand ways. It is conveyed as they face change, uncertainty, or threat, as they forgive or withhold forgiveness, as they reach out for or accept the gifts of the universe.

It was common a generation or two ago for parents to drop their children at Sunday school, CCD, or Hebrew school while the parents themselves seldom if ever partook of the life of the religious community. I hear less of this today, but perhaps that is a reflection of my particular context. Perhaps it is still more common than I would like to believe. I do, however, know families, two-parent families, in which the parents take turns bringing their children to church on Sunday mornings, while Mom and Dad, each in turn, has a quiet morning at home.

Such behavior clearly grows out of the assumption that it is the children's direct experience that is of value, with little appreciation for the power of religious community to shape the faith the parents in turn pass on to the children. It is my conviction that bringing children to participate in religious community is a positive aspect of their nurture. It is my conviction that the parents' own participation in religious community is just as important to the religious nurture of the children.

There was a young couple who attended our church for a short time with their infant son. They had recently come to our community, having moved far from their extended families and supportive network of friends. They had not been churchgoers, but in their aloneness were seeking a circle of friendship and support. The husband was working long hours, including many weekends. The wife was at home with the baby. Their participation at church ebbed as quickly as it had risen, but we do not know the reason. They did not leave us for another church, but for the secular lifestyle. Perhaps the habit of churchgoing simply had never really taken hold. Perhaps there was some other reason.

We do know that the wife was having a difficult time: the cabin fever of the at-home parent, plus some disillusionments in life, relationships with people who had been unreliable, deceptive, or manipulative. She was losing some of her faith in life, her faith in goodness, and was becoming cynical. We made attempts to reach out and to be of help, but somehow the connections were not successful. I worry that our church may have failed this family. I worry about the wife wrestling with such real and challenging spiritual issues. I worry especially about the child who, in his innocence, may be absorbing attitudes of negativity, cynicism, and mistrust. The church community might have cushioned and redirected the parents' growing sense of alienation, grounding them in a more positive way, thus helping them to feed their son with a more life-affirming attitude.

The church is not a cure-all for disillusionment and despair, but it can, I believe, counter such attitudes. Its most profound message is the message of hope, but more powerful than this articulated message is the lived reality of goodness found in healthy congregations—the best corrective of all. Religious community can be a source of strength and meaning for parents, and through them for children, if they will let it be so.

Before I leave this portion of the discussion, I would like to say just a few words about the parents' obligation to choose their religious community carefully. Not all churches and synagogues are created equal. Some welcome and nurture children and families more effectively than others. It is the parents' responsibility to search and explore, to be thoughtful about the criteria by which they wish to measure the possible religious communities, and only then to make their choice.

It would be understandable if, after two or three disappointing experiences, parents were to abandon the search and determine that churchgoing is not for them. It is my hope that parents will not become easily discouraged, but that they will persevere. Having urged a search for the best possible religious community, I must also urge parents not to set their expectations unattainably high. Every congregation has a weakness of some kind.

Having made a choice, the parental work is still not accomplished. They must then be prepared to become immersed in the life of that community, to sustain its strengths and to be a force in addressing its weaknesses. The healthiest congregations are made so not just by their professional leadership, but by the active participation of the laity. Parents must not simply turn over to the church or temple the work of their children's religious education, but must become partners in that work, teaching, supporting, critiquing (with love and respect), and enriching.

The
Home

~

When I was a child there was in our living room a particular print, a simple print in muted colors, of a young girl sitting on a bench beneath a tree, gazing at a bird on a low branch, the bird gazing back at her. The girl's posture was graceful and totally relaxed. It suggested an openness and receptivity; there was a communion between her and the bird. It was a restful picture, conveying peace, trust, harmony, wholeness of life. I wouldn't have used those words as a child, of course, but I often found myself drawn to the picture and soothed by it. This picture imprinted on my developing soul an image of life as gentle and good. In its profound, nonverbal way it called me to see my human life as connected to something beyond the human experience. It helped to ground and shape my faith.

Parents are the primary religious educators and the home is the center of religious development. Although the larger religious community is an essential component in growing a lasting faith—for both parents and children—the home, especially in the early years, is where the child's living unfolds, where meanings and values are rooted, where both crises and celebrations are most likely to occur.

There is an emotional power in the home that gives added weight and depth to the lessons learned there. Home is where we are known and accepted for who we are, in all our flawed human frailty. It is where we are loved and cherished, not for what we do, but for who we are, and so it is in the home that we are most open and receptive. (We know that not all homes are places of acceptance and safety, but trust that those parents who choose this book are loving, affirming parents. We leave for another time and place the discussion of spiritual nurture in homes where judgment and instability prevail.)

There is much in every home that conveys religious or spiritual meanings, but in this, as in so many other ways, parents in this time must bring a particular clarity and determination to shape their home life in centered, comforting, uplifting ways. In this, as in so many other spheres, popular culture pulls us away from deep, strengthening ways of being "at home."

Jobs and enrichment activities for both children and parents take family members outside of the home for longer and longer stretches of time. Much of the "homemaking" that was once done by parents is now done by decorators, cleaning services, and take-out food establishments. Certainly there is no inherent harm in using such services, but there is great harm in neglecting the atmosphere of the home and the opportunities for enhancing the spiritual life there in your own individual ways.

Attitudes in the home are conveyed to children every day—attitudes of patience, respect, affection, generosity, hospitality, deep listening, an open heart and mind. Art and other images in the home also convey values and spiritual meanings, both subtle and explicit. Green plants, bowls of shells or rocks, mobiles or wind chimes to catch the movement of the air, windows open to a garden beyond—all of these bespeak a spirituality.

Aesthetics of color and music, balance, and harmony help to convey a spiritual mood, but not all of us are artists in this way. Images can, however, be deliberately chosen. Paintings, posters, and other kinds of images may surround the child with feelings of gentleness and safety and call the child to ideals of peace and justice, or they may convey anger, cynicism, even fear. They may set a tone of warmth and beauty or of harshness and danger.

The careful display of artwork by family members and friends, and especially by the children, honors the stories and sensitivity of people we know and love. It honors and empowers the spiritual vision and imagination inherent in each individual, not just in professionals and authorities. *Careful display* means something more than ragged sheets held to the fridge with magnets. Children's drawings simply mounted on a backing of construction paper become works of art. Selected drawings properly framed and hung are a delight to the eyes and a spiritual gift to the whole family. Poems or stories neatly printed on quality paper with a special border become messages to meditate upon.

Handiwork—needlepoint, embroidery, quilted pieces—have an organic life and energy. Batik, stained glass, ceramics, and hand-tooled woodenware, shaped by human hands, not by megamachines, have warmth and authenticity. Arts and artifacts from around the world honor the diversity of the human spirit. Often they lift up different ways of understanding both the human and the holy. A certain sophistication or perfection may be sacrificed, but something so much richer is gained.

I shudder when I enter a home equipped with every technological gadget but devoid of any images that connect with the earth, with the larger circle of humanity, or with the mystery beyond. But to be in a home with seeds sprouting on the windowsills, patchwork cushions on the couch, books and pictures and little "collections" everywhere, enlivens and excites and awakens curiosity.

And then there are the sacred places in the home. With or without our support, children will find or create places where they feel safe and cozy—places where they can feel alone and can feel the beautiful, centering power of a private, personal spirituality. They may nest under a quilt; in a chair by a window to the night sky; under a card table, hidden by draped blankets; in a particular crook of a particular tree; behind the long drapes in the living room. Indoors or out, hidden or in view, they will find special nooks where they go to be quiet and alone.

They will also seek out shared places—the lap in the rocking chair, the parents' bed, curled on a cushion with the cat—safe, cozy, intimate places where the spirit is felt and fed. Wise parents are deliberate in protecting and honoring such sacred spaces.

Wise parents, tending to their own spiritual lives, will have their adult sacred places as well—comfortable, beautiful corners where the space itself invites them into a time of serenity. Perhaps a meaningful quote or poem will be posted, candles will be ready to light, music will be at hand. Perhaps there will be smooth stones to fondle, something beautiful to look at, a place to put a cup of tea. Let your children be your teachers in honoring the need to create sacred space.

Beyond the atmosphere of the home, parents can be deliberate in other ways as well. I would dwell here particularly on the role of ritual and prayer as intentional ways for parents to deepen both their own and their children's sense of faith. As will be discussed in the next chapter, there is a particular power to communal worship, a power created by the gathered energy of religious seekers. What can be offered in the home is not to replace the gathering in religious community. It is an intimate spiritual centering, blending into the daily life of the family, with the potential to respond to personal events, ebbs and flows, crises and celebrations.

Someone once said, "Ritual can help us to sense holiness, or the possibility of holiness, in the familiar." Ritual, the enactment of a symbolic pattern, with gesture, song, and candles, is a potent way to evoke or to express deep feelings, to focus and hold the mysteries, miracles, and heightened energies of our human journey. But don't be daunted by the idea that ritual must be elaborate or formal or precise. The best rituals are often the simplest. Sometimes they are designed with deliberation and thoughtfulness; sometimes they emerge organically in the life of a family.

When our children were young, we always lit candles at dinnertime, bringing a shimmer to the table, the dance of light and shadow, inviting the softer light to soften voices, and sometimes nerves and tempers. We always waited until everyone was at the table before we began to eat, affirming the mealtime as a time of togetherness, a time when each family member—and the family unit as well—was valued. And we tried to wait until everyone was finished before any of us left the table, thus slowing our pace, savoring those moments together in the midst of our scattered, busy lives. It didn't always work, of course, but most of the time it did. We never sat down and said, "Now how shall we structure dinner time to help us sense the holiness in our being together as a family?" If we had, we probably would have come up with something that felt contrived and silly. The ritual created itself.

The simple lighting of candles as a family sits down to dinner is a moment of pause, however brief, that affirms the significance of the gathering of the family and a sense of gratitude for the gifts of the earth that sustain us. Perhaps hands are held; perhaps words are spoken. It is the intentionality of pausing to sense the holy that is important, and the capturing of that pause in some physical way that embodies it and makes it more real.

This is the sense in which the ritual of the Sabbath is honored in Jewish homes, a time set apart to enjoy the simple pleasures of life, to know and to appreciate the gifts of God's creation—children, family, good food, music, poetry, a walk in the country—to feel the holiness in the everyday. The Jewish Sabbath is rich with ritual—the lighting of candles, the gestures, the familiar prayers and songs. The blessing of the children at the Sabbath dinner is a particularly wonderful moment. The Hebrew scriptures say, "Remember the Sabbath day, to keep it holy." Wilfred Cantwell Smith, historian of religion, says, "Remember the Sabbath day to understand holiness."

Some rituals we inherit from our religious tradition, others emerge organically in the flow of family life, and others we design more deliberately. Two families in my congregation shaped rituals around the time of winter solstice, but in very different ways. One family, on the shortest day of the year, would refrain from turning on any electric lights in their home. "Let the dark be dark," they said. Let us not mask or deny this natural season in the turning of the earth, but face it with bravery and even gladness. They would light candles and oil lamps as needed, but in this simple, almost primitive way, they would mark a moment most of us pass by without notice.

In the other family, the season of darkness was marked beginning a full month before the date of the solstice. At dusk the family lit one candle on that first night of their personal celebration. On the second night they lit two candles, on the third night three and so on until, when the solstice arrived the living room was bright with candles, countering the darkness, but even in that countering there was a ritual acknowledgment. Each day following the solstice this family lit one less candle, and by the time they were back to lighting just a single candle, and then none, the natural light was returning and they no longer felt the need for extra brightness.

Simple gestures sanctify that which matters most. Seasons of the earth are often occasion for religious observance. So are seasons of the soul, major life passages of birth, growth, transformation, and death.

It was February when my mother-in-law, Muttie, died. My children were ten and fourteen. We gathered the extended family together, shared our memories, laughed and cried, and planned the memorial service. We grieved and then moved on in our lives. A year later, as the date of Muttie's death neared, I found myself buying fresh flowers, which Muttie had always loved and often indulged in. For me it was an unusual indulgence, but I needed to mark the anniversary of her death, to embody this next stage of mourning. "Muttie flowers" my children called them, and again we talked of her and remembered and cried a little more. "Muttie flowers" became an important annual ritual in our home, a visible symbol, a prompting to remember and to honor our sadness at this loss from our family circle.

Another family, grieving the death of a young man, father of two young daughters, began to bring a special candle to every family gathering—birthdays, Thanksgiving, Christmas, summer barbecues. Whenever and wherever the extended family gathered, they lit "Paul's candle," and his presence was with them.

Formal wakes, memorial services, and funerals are important communal gatherings at the time of loss and grief, but they are usually wordy occasions. These simpler rituals, based in the family and the home, are more physical than verbal, and thus are more accessible to the spiritual lives of both children and adults.

Children themselves have a natural bent for creating rituals. They will create patterns of steps to be used in approaching schools and verses that must be said whenever the car passes a black dog. There is a fine line between the kind of magical thinking they may attach to some of these behaviors and the heightening of sensitivities that is the gift of spiritually attuned rituals. The blue sweater they wore when they won the spelling bee or the route to the ballpark they took the day they hit the home run may be meaningless charms, or perhaps moving through these patterns focuses their energies in an empowering way. Let your children be the leaders in the rituals of your family life. Note where they are already enacting ritualistic behaviors and you may find areas of their lives that are potent for them, unbeknownst to you.

The sensory richness of ritual has its particular way of opening the heart, but spoken prayers can also function as ritual, both in the repetitive familiarity of selected phrases or verses and in words chosen freshly for a particular moment. Our religious traditions are rich with prayers that have served people well for thousands of years, some of them memorized and repeated daily, weekly, seasonally year after year. Their familiarity and their association with the gentle safety of the childhood years can make them deep sources of comfort and consolation.

I talked once with a woman who had been raised as an Episcopalian but had left that faith behind in her early adulthood. For several decades she found her religious meaning and comfort elsewhere, but when faced with a crisis in her life and a crying need to lean on a spiritual source of strength, she found herself saying the prayers of her Episcopalian childhood, prayers she had not even thought about for thirty years or more. She no longer believed the words she was saying, but they rose in her heart and to her lips, and she found comfort in the familiarity of the ritual.

The embedding of prayers in the hearts and minds of our children can be part of the gift of faith we hand on to them, but the habit of praying should be embraced with some caveats.

Polly Berrien Berends, in her book *Gently Lead*, tells this story:

When my mother was a little girl her father always said grace at the beginning of meals. When she was older one day her father said, "Now, Mary, you are a big girl. You lead us in grace today."

Awed and thrilled, my mother took a deep breath, folded her hands, bowed her head and said boldly something like:

"Blmphsgifthrlsrifledgsmthrpflgnrsblskhfamen."

Immediately she was sent from the table.

After the meal my grandmother went to my mother's room. "Mary," she said, "Why on earth did you do such a disrespectful thing? How could you? Whatever possessed you?"

My mother had no idea what she had done wrong. All those years she had listened to her father pray, and he had done it so fast that she had never heard anything but nonsense. She had never had any idea that anything meaningful was being said.

In like manner, we often hear stories of children's mishearing the words of oft-repeated prayers. "Our Father who art in heaven, Harold be thy name." The simple saying of prayers is not enough. The prayers must be intelligible to the children, they must carry a meaning that is relevant to their lives, and they must reflect a healthy, affirming theology.

Table graces and bedtime prayers are already common in many homes, offering that moment of pause, of creating sacred time and space. All praise to those families who have woven these threads into the fabric of their children's lives. I would simply offer the caution that these times of prayer should be used with care and intentionality to be sure the sentiments expressed are true to the family's deepest beliefs, rather than a lazy echoing of prayers that come easily to hand.

"Now I lay me down to sleep. I pray the Lord my soul to keep. If I should die before I wake, I pray the Lord my soul to take." This is a classic, easy standby. It may echo the true faith of some families, but if it doesn't reflect the spiritual meanings you want your child to hold deep in his or her heart, then don't use it casually. Is the possibility of imminent death the notion you want your child to take into sleep? Is the image of God as "Lord," with all the feelings of maleness and mastery attached to it, the image you wish to sponsor?

Many of the old traditional prayers are elegant in their imagery and cadence. They are poetic and, like all good poetry, may elicit a deep and tender response. With that model before us, it is understandable that some of us feel intimidated by the idea of creating our own prayers. But the true expressions of our hearts, though they may be plainly put, have an emotional power that derives from their depth and authenticity.

To be thoughtful about the prayers used with children, parents must begin with an honest reflection on their own theological understanding—to whom or to what is the prayer to be addressed? Does one hold a faith in a personal God "out there," or is one's concept of the divine more amorphous? Traditional forms of prayer lead us into the pattern of "talking to" and assume a personal kind of theism. This is the style and language most familiar in the public sphere, the style you and your child probably experience in church or temple.

At home you need not feel constrained to replicate this form of prayer, but you should be thoughtful about the theological assumptions from which your prayer flows so that it will have a clarity and integrity. If your private ways of prayer differ markedly from what your child experiences at church, at some point you will want to talk about that and help your child understand how the two are linked. The goal is to see that what happens at home and what happens at church are mutually reinforcing, rather than diverging or confusing.

There is no one right way to pray. When there are no prayers at hand, or when the words of others feel stilted or distanced from your own reality, then is the time to extemporize from the heart, trusting that, although the words may not be poetry, they will be honest and true. When you feel moved to put into words a profound sense of gratitude or compassion, or even of anguish; when you feel a sincere need for forgiveness or guidance or healing; when you are holding someone else's well-being in your heart; when the human sources of support are insufficient, then simply speak that truth.

James Carse, professor of the history and literature of religion at New York University, has said, "It is not the content of the heart that matters, only the ability to speak from it. . . . What is truly spoken from the heart is prayer . . . in an encounter with divine reality we do not hear a voice, but acquire a voice."

Prayers that are genuine and heartfelt convey a spiritually potent intimacy and authenticity, especially when children hear their parents pray in their own words. And they will learn that each individual has a spiritual integrity within him or herself. Each individual, parents as well as children, can feel and express a worthy spiritual message.

Prayer is an amazingly rich resource in the spiritual lives of both adults and children, but it need not always be expressed in words. Its full breadth and depth cannot be fully realized if we continue to think of it only as the spoken word, addressed to a transcendent God, using a formalized kind of vocabulary.

Simple forms of centering or meditation invite a stilling of our busy minds and welcome a clarifying and restorative peace. Kathleen Norris, while working as an artist in residence in elementary schools, sometimes invited the children to make a great noise—and then to make silence. It was a grand exercise, surprising and challenging to children unused to a time of silence simply for its own sake. Norris found that the children's creativity and imagination were freer emerging from the time of silence. Their written responses to the silence were poetic and often prayerful. "Silence is spiders spinning their webs, it's like a silkworm making its silk. Lord, help me to know when to be silent," one child wrote. And another, "Silence reminds me to take my soul with me wherever I go."

There are teachers who engage their classes in centering exercises at the beginning of each morning and find that the time used in this way is more than made up by the greater focus and clarity the children bring to their work throughout the rest of the day. In the home parents might want to introduce moments of deliberative, focused silence, in lieu of mealtime or bedtime prayers perhaps, or when the family regathers at the end of the day—a moment of silence, before news is shared, simply to be glad to be together.

There is the silence of meditation, and then there is the silence of contemplative prayer, deepening into a connection with the holy spark within one's own being. I have found this form of prayer to be easily accessible to children, the opening of oneself to the presence of the holy, the presence of the spirit of life. In contemplative prayer one deepens into a centered awareness of the spiritual essence that is always present within us and around us, lets that energy flame brightly, and simply rests in the power and beauty of feeling oneself a part of something alive and mysterious.

Sometimes words get in the way and what is needed is wordless prayer. Sometimes words are inadequate for the depths of our feeling and knowing. In the religious life, the spiritual life, there is much that is real beyond question, yet elusive. Not only are words insufficient but they distract from and distort the reality of our participation in the mysterious, holy energy of life.

As Brother Lawrence, a seventeenth-century monk, said, "Prayer is the practice of the presence of God." In contemplative prayer one invites the presence of God into one's heart, or more accurately, invites one's own attention to that presence that is already there. And then one may simply rest in that sustaining, healing, holding presence. One may simply rest in that presence, or may bring to it the cares, questions, fears, longings, and loves of one's heart and soul. One may bring these, not to be resolved, but again simply to be held.

This form of prayer assumes that the holy lives within us at least as much as it lives beyond us. It is directed to the spirit within oneself, rather than to a god apart from oneself. Rabbi Marcia Prager writes,

> Torah tells us that at Sinai, when Moshe spoke to God, God answered him, 'b'kol,' with sound or perhaps even 'with voice,' . . . Moshe, the rabbis say, heard God speak 'b'kol shel Moshe,' with Moshe's own voice! He heard God's voice as his own voice. He heard from the inside out!

Still other forms of meditation call us to a heightened mindfulness of all that is already around us, present in each moment of each day. They call us to be fully present. There are many ways we might design mindful, prayerful moments for our children, inviting their attention to the breath, for instance, or to the sounds of the night. At mealtime we might invite a moment of full silent attention to the sensory richness of the foods—their colors, textures, tastes, even sounds. Take a slice of melon or an orange or a kiwi and really encounter it fully. It is a prayer.

As in ritual, our children can be our teachers in such mindfulness. Their natural capacity to attend to the patterns of clouds, or leaves against the sky, the sparkle of each grain of sand, the feel of ice cream in their mouths or kitten fur against their cheeks, the glorious ooze of mud, can call us to a prayerful, spiritual response to the majesty of the ordinary.

I remember a springtime outing to a bog with the children and parents of my congregation, an outing on which our guide advised that we should wear boots. I took this to mean boots were recommended because woods and other wild areas in New Hampshire are usually muddy in the spring, but it had been dry for several weeks. The woods around my house were dry, so I didn't wear boots on this late April outing. Big mistake. Regardless of how dry the season, one should always wear boots in the bog, which is like a sponge, holding vast quantities of water.

Through this particular bog there were laid wooden planks for visitors to walk upon. These planks sink when you step upon them, and the water rises up. The planks prevent you from sinking into the mud but do not keep your feet dry. And I hadn't worn my boots. My sneakers and feet were quickly soaked; I was becoming quite irritable.

But just in front of me on this single file walk through the bog were a young father and his son, three-year-old Ian—also wearing sneakers, not boots. Ian could barely contain himself, so delighted was he with his wet sneakers, the oozing mud, the missteps off the planks into deeper muck. The father could hardly restrain Ian from immersing himself face first in this glory of warm, smelly, squishy mess. What Ian kept saying, as he splashed, was, "This is so fun! This is so fun!" While I worried about wet feet and dirty sneakers, Ian was prayerfully present to the wonders of the moment and became my teacher.

Children can be our teachers as well in lifting up the disciplines of movement meditation. Adults schedule sessions for yoga, tai chi, or sacred circle dancing. Children need no teachers to know the centering, exhilarating rewards of swinging, spinning, and balancing their way along a wall. So much of this is so natural, but with a consciousness and a naming it could become even more potent in a family's life.

Prayer is the practice of the presence of God, and prayer itself requires practice. Whether it is spoken prayer, a quieting of the mind, or a heightened awareness that we wish to introduce into our family's lifestyle, let us acknowledge that we may not be good at it at first. Like most skills—ice-skating, piano playing, computer programming—these spiritual forms also require practice. We may have an innate impulse or inclination toward the spirit, but it is only with repetition and determination that those impulses can become smooth, easy, and effective in our lives and the lives of our children.

Prayer and ritual can take many forms, and in your own home and family you have great freedom to adopt and even create forms that feel most appropriate and comfortable to you. (Some rituals, prayers, and meditations are offered in this book, beginning on page 105.) Prayer at home has the added benefit of being adaptable to the particularities of the moment, responsive to difficulties as they arise, and reflective of your child's particular personality and needs.

The Religious
Community

~

When I was a child, the circle of family, friends, church, and teachers was a nearly seamless whole. But as I became an adolescent, that small, safe, coherent world was left behind as my family moved first to one small city, then a year later to another. Now there was one circle of friends and acquaintances in the neighborhood, another circle at school, yet another circle at church. These were difficult years. Adolescence, at best, is a difficult time. Moving from the simple rural life to the complex, sophisticated city, then moving again, multiplied the stress.

When I was an adolescent, the places I felt safest and most able to be myself were in my church communities. Perhaps this was in part because I had already learned a deep sense of connection to and trust in the church. Perhaps it was because these churches were designed as places of acceptance and love. Perhaps it was because the people there truly liked me and my peers just as we were, with all our annoying teenage traits.

The church school teacher who took us to visit neighboring churches when we were in the seventh grade also took us out for coffee (lots of milk and sugar) and doughnuts after every visit and talked with us as though he really enjoyed it. The woman who taught our eighth grade class was as old as the hills and as sweet as sunshine. She knew we found the class deadly dull and could barely wait to break away and go sit at the soda fountain in the drugstore next door—and she forgave us and loved us anyway.

In the Christian scriptures, when Jesus is asked when the kingdom of God will arrive, he replies, "The kingdom of God is not coming . . . [it] is among you." For generations this was translated as "The kingdom of God is *within* you," but more recent scholarship renders it as "among." The inner spiritual life is profound, indeed, but the spiritual energy, the fullness of life, experienced in relationship or in community, may be even greater.

Jesus also said, "Where two or three are gathered in my name, there am I in the midst of them." Whether it be in Jesus' name or not, where two or three gather in the name of religion, in the name of spirituality, in the name of holiness, a sacred spark, a living flame, will be alight in their midst. Where two or three are gathered—not simply as a congenial group or for some functional purpose but in all the honesty and depth and beauty of the truest self—where two or three are gathered in such integrity and wholeness, there is the religious moment, the religious place.

The Community of Worship

We have reflected on the spiritual moments that occur to children spontaneously in the course of their daily lives and on the ways in which family and home life can sponsor feelings of reverence, connection, and centered stillness. These intimate forms of worship may be rich and deep, but they can be even fuller in the mysterious energy of gathered community. There, other voices and visions can further enrich and enliven the worship experience. There, the stories and the wisdom of other lives and ancient traditions may express spiritual insights with a clarity and energy that can uncover further layers of meaning or can refresh a conviction that might feel tired and stale. There, the potency of worship becomes heightened.

The blending of voices in song and in liturgy adds energy to the worship experience, as does the touch of our neighbor's hand in greeting. But it is not just this obvious kind of connection. I have heard others say that even in stretches of silent meditation or prayer, centering within oneself while sitting in community, there are a power and a grace that transcend the experience of such silent meditation or prayer in solitude. I have experienced this myself. The very presence of others is felt, and one is held and supported in some mysterious unspoken way.

We all, children and adults, need acceptance and affirmation. We need it first in the family's embrace, but as we grow and expand we need to find it in other places and faces as well. We need affirmation of what we do, validating our skills and talents, but on a deeper level, we need to be accepted simply for who we are. In schools and workplaces, and indeed in most spheres of society, it is our doing and achieving that is affirmed. In worship it is the whole self that is engaged and embraced.

We need a sanctuary, a safe place, to open the tender true center of who we are, to open it to ourselves as well as to others. Good, healthy communal worship offers such a sanctuary, a place made safe by the shared needs and trust of the worshippers there and by the covenant they make with one another. Sometimes this covenant is explicit. In my congregation we say in unison each Sunday an affirmation that we will be loving, accepting, and peaceful with one another. But even when such a covenant is not spoken, in a healthy, nurturing congregation it is implicit. The religious community is a cherishing community, especially in the hour of worship when we are most engaged with the holy spirit of life; it is a time and place of safety. We can be authentically who we are, and we will be accepted as we are, "warts and all," as someone once said.

In religious community we are held and affirmed, but we are not the center of attention. To be in community is humbling. It is to be one among many, and it is a corrective to the kind of egocentric spirituality that can grow if we encounter the holy only in private ways. Humility is a deeply spiritual quality—not self-abasement or denigration, but understanding the self as an integrated piece of the larger circle of humanity, indeed of all of life. It is to understand oneself as singularly beautiful and significant— as every other person is also singularly beautiful and significant.

What I particularly want to lift up here is the way that children's faith is deepened and strengthened when they worship alongside their parents and other adults. In some religious communities the children worship separately from the adults. There is value to this pattern, to be sure, but I find deeper value in shared intergenerational worship, in which children can see and feel that adults are receptive to and moved by the spirit. It is the modeling of adults that will take root deeply in the children's own being. In this, as in other spheres of their development, it is not what they are told, but what they witness that shapes their growth.

But you may think "children can't sit still; they are uncomfortable with the quiet; they can't sustain their focus through a worship experience of more than a few minutes at the most." I have occasion to officiate at wedding ceremonies and memorial services, not only for members of my own congregation, but also for people of the larger community—sometimes for people who are "unchurched"; sometimes for families whose members are from diverse religious traditions. Often there are children at these ceremonies, and their behavior varies widely. Sometimes the children constantly fidget, wander away from their seats, and are obviously disinterested in the event, which holds deep emotional significance for the adults. Other times the children sit for an hour or more, attentive, engaged, comfortable with themselves and with the church setting.

The difference, of course, has to do with their exposure to such settings, their understanding of what it is all about, and the expectations of their parents or other adult companions. When children attend worship regularly, with clear expectations of what to expect, and with good adult modeling, they become comfortable in that setting and receptive to the gifts it has to offer.

For many years in my congregation in New Hampshire I led "centering" times with the children, beginning at kindergarten age. In these centering times we stretched, loosened our bodies, breathed deeply, and opened to the magical mystery of the energy of life flickering within us all the time. We would soften our eyes, and I would guide the reflections of the children toward their inner knowing, toward deep feelings of love, gratitude, compassion, and safety. We would sit quietly, with soft music playing for several minutes—meditating, praying.

When I first launched this centering experience, to tell the truth, it felt like a disastrous failure. The children snickered and rolled their eyes and giggled and nudged one another. This kind of experience was new to them. They were uncomfortable and embarrassed. Perhaps they thought they would "do it wrong." And, to tell the truth, I didn't really do it very well myself at first. I had to learn a great deal about timing and about simplicity, not cluttering those times with stories or lessons, with too many images or too much direction. For a whole year I persisted despite the apparent futility of the endeavor.

There were times when I was tempted to abandon the project altogether, but something within me felt sure that there was an unfulfilled potential here, and I persevered.

The second year it was a little better, and by the third year it was clear that some genuine spiritual, centering experiences were happening, some worshipful moments—not for every child, and not every time, but for many of them, much of the time. There sometimes was a palpable stillness in the room. The children sometimes were slow to reopen their eyes and focus again on the energies beyond themselves when the meditation time ended. As the process became familiar and comfortable for them, and perhaps as they felt my own faith in the promise of this experience, they relaxed into it, opened to it, and were fed by it.

Too often we—parents, ministers, and religious educators—cast our expectations of what children can and cannot experience too low. If we think they can't sit still for several minutes, if we think their attention span requires a change of stimulation and pace every twenty seconds, this will become a self-fulfilling prophecy. But if we expect that they have the capacity for serious meditation and prayer, for deep spiritual feelings and impulses, even complex spiritual thoughts, we may find that indeed this is true.

We might not want them to sit regularly in hour-long services cast in complex, sophisticated language, but that is not the only option for meaningful intergenerational worship. As parents search critically for a religious community for their family, they will want to attend carefully to, among other things, the ways of worship for children.

The Community of Care

For me the words of a particular beloved old chant lift up the heart and soul of religious community. "*Ubi caritas et amor, ubi caritas, deus ibi est.*" "Where there is kindness and love, God is there."

Over the years I have often had occasion to ask adults what they remember of their own childhood experiences in church or temple. Rarely do they remember the content of particular lessons. Sometimes they remember ceremonial, ritualistic moments or social occasions. Almost always they remember particular people—ministers, priests, rabbis, religious education teachers, choir directors, pillars of the church or synagogue with whom they interacted in one way or another. Sometimes, tragically, these are harsh memories—instances when they were chastised or excluded or even mocked. More often (hallelujah!) they are warm memories of adults who welcomed, soothed, or affirmed them.

These one-on-one human connections are the most formative in children's lives, and when they occur in religious community they have a particular potency because of that spiritual context. When the religious communities we turn to are safe and healthy, we allow ourselves to be more open and vulnerable there, and so we can be touched in deeper places. We are more ready to trust, and although our children may not understand any of this, they do sense their parents' moods and they learn to bring that same receptivity and sensitivity to their attendance at church or temple.

Beyond the family, the religious community may feel like the only safe and appropriate place for personal concerns and significant life passages to be shared. It is in religious community that birth and death, marriages and ceremonies of holy union are marked. It is in religious community that illness and healing, despair and hope may be held with tender concern. These life transformations are spiritual events, needing spiritual as well as practical support, needing to be marked with ritual and prayer, song and celebration.

A particularly profound element in many contemporary worship gatherings is the sharing of the personal concerns of members of the congregation. This is done in various ways—sometimes by written concerns spoken by the worship leader in the time of pastoral prayer; sometimes with the lighting of candles; sometimes spoken by the individuals themselves.

In my New Hampshire congregation, the Sharing of Joys and Concerns was an emotionally charged piece of every Sunday morning's worship. When one family celebrated the adoption of a new baby, every other adopted child (and adult) sitting in the sanctuary felt affirmed. When a young woman tearfully told of her miscarriage, her five-year-old son standing by her side may not have fully understood the meaning of what she shared, but he surely knew that his mother was deeply sad and that now others would reach out to comfort her.

Terminal illnesses, deaths, and other deeply painful passages were often noted in the Joys and Concerns. There were parents who thought it inappropriate for the children to hear about these disturbing dimensions of life. But I submit that children hear of these anyway, too often in secretive whispers, as sensationalized news stories, in flat, pragmatic ways, or with unbounded anguish. In the church community, when people speak about the deaths and divorces and incapacitating circumstances they face, the children hear these as honest realities of the human journey. They hear them not as shameful secrets or meaningless tragedies to be endured, but as deep, tender pains that are at least partially eased when they are shared in this circle of loving care.

In this context, as the children are offered the opportunity to express their own celebrations and griefs as well, they learn to be vulnerable and find that strength is extended to them when they open their hearts and tell the truths of their lives. They learn to be both receivers and givers of the gift of compassion.

A particularly beloved twenty-year-old young man of our congregation was tragically killed in an automobile accident. At his memorial service there was an open opportunity for anyone who wished to speak to do so. When that moment came, although there were dozens of youth and adults in the congregation who were bursting with stories and feelings, there was a long, slow silence. And, then, it was ten-year-old Katie who finally came forward to tell of how David had befriended her, and of her affection for him. She opened the gates for the many, many who followed with their reminiscences.

When my own brother died and the condolences came from every quarter, the words and the cards of the children, with their freshness and honesty, were especially touching. *Ubi caritas, deus ibi est.* Caring was extended and I felt held in a spiritual net of comfort—a net that was both human and divine.

There is a long and remarkable tradition of church members bringing cakes and casseroles to a family in trouble. Casseroles, transportation to medical appointments, a little extra cash in particular circumstances, respite care, chores and errands—all these practical forms of help are realities in religious communities, and they can make a profound difference for individuals or families, especially those who do not have the support of extended family nearby. Whether it is articulated or not, the casseroles and other forms of help carry emotional support as well.

Anne Lamott, in her poignant biographical work *Traveling Mercies,* describes how the women of her church helped her as she was expecting her first child and was alone in that time. "When I was at the end of my rope," she says, "the people at St. Andrew tied a knot in it for me and helped me hold on." Every outreach to a single mother or father, or to any of the many forms families may take, is an outreach to the children as well. When parents are supported, the children are supported. The knot in the rope helps everyone to hold on.

The Community of Social Justice

There is a certain myth of childhood that would have us believe that children are selfish and egocentric. This myth is bolstered by well-founded research and analysis in the area of human development, scholarship that describes the inescapably egocentric nature of children. Although I believe absolutely in the integrity of that research and resulting theory, still there is much anecdotal evidence that celebrates the depths of compassion and generosity of children of all ages. I think that in some paradoxical way both these ways of understanding children's capacity to be empathic are true. Children are developmentally incapable of seeing things from any perspective other than their own. And they do sense sadness and loneliness in others; they do give, sometimes sacrificially; they understand and are angered by injustice.

Those who take the spiritual life seriously must also take seriously the religious imperative to do good in the world and this is as true for children as it is for adults. Nadine Gordimer, the great South African novelist, has written, "The true definition of loneliness is lack of social responsibility." There are too many lonely people among us, and much of that loneliness is due not to lack of companionship, but to the lack of deep compassionate connections. It is not the presence or absence of others that creates loneliness, but the state of our own spirit. To feel lonely is to feel impoverished, depleted, empty, alienated, and disconnected. We are in danger of raising another generation of lonely people, of people who feel self-sufficient, responsible to and for only themselves. To be connected, to feel the thread of connection, not just to one or two intimates, but to humanity, is to know also one's responsibility—and to be glad in it.

Opportunities for social service abound. Schools, scouts, and other organizations urge our children to action, and it is good that they develop the practice of service in many ways. The theological meaning of social justice work in religious community, however, gives them an added importance. In the mosques, temples, and churches of our society, the deep reality of our spiritual kinship with all of humankind is celebrated. We extend ourselves in service, not out of a sense of obligation, but out of a sense of our inherent interconnectedness. "He ain't heavy. He's my brother," as the song says. We feed the hungry not because we should, but because we want to.

It is well-known that we can find in all the major religions of the world the teaching "Do unto others as you would have them do unto you." Although the phrasing may differ, the essence of the teaching runs through all faiths. Likewise the proverb "Under the sky all people are one family" is a part of the folk wisdom of all people. These are basic, focusing religious teachings that become embodied in many ways in religious community.

The spirituality of ancient, earth-based traditions celebrating our interconnectedness with the earth and with all of life with an equal passion is recently re-awakened in some contemporary religious communities. It is not only humankind to whom we are to extend our care, but also the egret, the great white whale, and the mountain laurel, caring for our fragile planet as we care for the fragile children of the Romanian orphanages.

There is theological integrity to the social justice work of faith communities. There is also the opportunity there for people of all ages to work side by side, making soup for the soup kitchens, writing letters to elected officials, painting banners for a peace march, cleaning the plot of land for a playground.

In religious community children can put their own hands to the task of social justice work, but they can also see in a very immediate way that the adults they most respect are also doing that work. My present congregation is preparing a Community Garden, working collaboratively with a local synagogue. We will give the produce from this vegetable garden to a local soup kitchen. The children of our two congregations will work alongside their parents and other adults, preparing the soil, planting, weeding, harvesting, and delivering the vegetables to their destination. They will soak up the sun, get their hands dirty, make some new friends, and see in a graphic and colorful way the contributions they are making to the health and well-being of their neighbors.

There is a story—perhaps apocryphal—from the peace movement of the sixties. A child was asked if she believed that peace really was possible, and she replied, "Of course there will be peace, because my mother and father go to a meeting every Wednesday night to work with other adults so that peace will come." To a child, if well-meaning adults are working on an issue, of course it will be resolved. Of course peace will come and the world will be saved. What an affirming, faith-supporting kind of message those parents conveyed to their child.

In one of those wonderful cyclical patterns, spiritual strength and richness derive from the giving of oneself and also lead to the giving of oneself. The justice work of religious communities deepens souls even as it lightens burdens.

Held in Community

The energies of worship, loving care, and social action are not separate energies, but are woven together in religious community in ways that are mutually strengthening and enlivening. A child once said, "We inched a little closer to God, and because we did, we became a little better ourselves."

In recent years we have heard so often, and in so many contexts, the phrase "it takes a village to raise a child." Nowhere is it more true than in discussion of the religious nurture of children. Community is a central piece of this nurture for many reasons: for the support and ongoing religious education of the parents, as discussed in chapter four; for the embodiment and transmission of tradition, ritual, and story; for the modeling and teaching offered by others in religious community.

But the most important reason is that to be a religious or spiritual being means to be in relationship with others. The central religious qualities of love and care become real only as they are lived, tested, deepened in community. Compassion and forgiveness are meaningless in the abstract. They are learned only in part through lessons. They are learned fully through life, through the experience of being cared for and of being accepted and held even when we have been weak or wrong or hurtful. They are learned by being among others whose hearts and minds are truly open to one another. They are learned as we are coached and held accountable for such virtues, as we are expected to live them out.

I know a family that was deeply involved in a church community for several years. Their children attended the church school and the parents went to adult education programs, tending to their own spiritual nurture as well as being responsible church workers. As the children grew into the increasingly busy years of middle childhood and the mother returned to work, their lives grew more and more crowded and stressed. One day they decided to simplify by withdrawing from church and guiding their children's religious education at home. These are thoughtful, sensitive parents, clear and sure about their own faith, and I'm sure that if anyone could do an adequate job of religious educating on their own, it is they.

Home schooling is increasing in our society, usually in response to dissatisfaction with the public school systems. A comparable dissatisfaction with religious education options may lead concerned parents in the direction of home religious education; or they may have other reasons. In some ways these parents might do an admirable job of shaping a program that meaningfully reflects their own faith. They might create lessons and rituals, tell stories, sing songs, talk of values, and share with their children deep meanings and messages from their own lives and the lives of others they admire. I would, in fact, encourage all parents to do just this—to be the primary religious educators of their own children. But I would also encourage parents to see this as only one dimension of the religious experience their children need and to support and supplement their homework with regular family involvement in a synagogue or church.

Religious community is not the only possible community, of course, but, when it is working as it should, it is where we are called to our best selves. It is where the ideals of human behavior are in our consciousness, where we expect to be loving and giving, and where we are expected to be loving and giving. In the marketplace, in the political sphere, on the highway, we are seldom called to live out the best that is in us. The prevailing forces of speed and greed, of self-interest call us to the same. The distinct quality of church life is that we go there not to accomplish something or get something, but simply to be and to become the finest, fullest, noblest selves we can become.

There is a story of a little girl who asked her parents, as they drove to church one Sunday morning, "What do we get at church?" In response to her parents' puzzled looks, she said, "At the library we get books; at the bank we get money; at the grocery store we get milk. What do we get at church?"

It is the wrong question, of course. Although in fact we may "get" much at church—strength, knowledge, challenge, spiritual insight, ethical clarification, moral support, healing, friendship—"getting" is not the appropriate intention to bring to this experience. Nor is the intention of "doing." Although in fact we may listen, talk, pray, think, sing, hug, and wash dishes, the "doing" is not the primary intention either.

In our society of agendas and tasks, action items and deliverables, religious community stands apart. We gather not to get, or to do, or to achieve, but simply to be, to be together in particular ways—ways of seeking and celebrating and supporting, ways of connecting, binding together the fragments of lives into a unified, centered whole, binding together the solitariness of individuals into the strength of community. The binding together is never complete, however. It is an ongoing process. This is what religious community is—process, beingness.

In religious community we may honor one another simply on the basis of the inherent worth and dignity, the inherent divinity, of each person. Then from religious community we must take this attitude back into the larger world in whatever small ways we can, chipping away at the barriers and indignities of public life, the deceptions and impatience of the marketplace. And as the indignities and injustices of those places begin to touch and tarnish us again, we need to return to communities of the spirit to be reminded of trust and of love, to be made whole and to remember the possibility of a world made whole.

John Westerhoff of the Divinity School at Duke University has said that "faith is communicated by participation in community of faith." In religious community both child and adult have their faith and their beliefs stretched through images and stories, thoughts and insights. Because the sacred will always remain just beyond, we will always need new and different ways to catch glimpses, to know in part, to draw closer. We need religious community for the fullness of celebration, for joining our voices in singing, and for the depth and energy that come in shared worship. And, we need the thinking of the community as a corrective to narrowness and distortions that are inevitable when one is left alone.

There are the practical supports of community as well. As I sat in my office one dreary winter afternoon, the telephone rang and I heard the barely audible voice of a ten-year-old member of my congregation. She had a problem and was frightened and didn't know what to do. By mistake, and I truly do believe that it was by mistake, she had written in a favorite book of her mother's, an expensive craft book her mother had lent her. She had compounded her error by trying to erase the writing and in the process had worn a hole in the page. What should she do? We talked about how it had happened and how she felt, and what her mother's response would likely be. I encouraged her to take the book to her mother with a truthful explanation and a heartfelt apology—and she did.

What a simple event!—and what a simple solution! The very ordinariness of the dilemma is what gives it its weight. Daily we each, children and adults, face such dilemmas and too often blunder through them alone, exaggerating and distorting them through our own narrow, unfocused lenses. What was powerful in this instance was that the child was embedded in a religious community that she knew would be understanding and accepting of her, but would also take such an ethical issue seriously. She knew and trusted an adult in that community to hear her story, to support and comfort her, but also to offer guidance.

It is a truism of child rearing, particularly through the teenage years, that young people need adults other than their parents to know and accept and guide them. No matter how understanding and wise their own parents are, there are times when young people need to talk to someone else, need to look to someone else's example. With grandparents and other adults of the extended family often hundreds or thousands of miles away, children have fewer and fewer opportunities to develop long-term relationships with adults other than their parents. Increasingly our neighborhoods, workplaces, and voluntary communities gather around particular age groups and lifestyles. One may relate to a coach for a season or a teacher for a year, but to know someone over years of change and growth is a special kind of knowing, and it is common in religious community.

These are great gifts of religious community—the mixing of generations and the enduring nature of relationships. The church or temple community is an ideal environment for fostering intimacy also because of the valuing of trust and care and relationship inherent in good religious community. Here there are likely to be shared values between the respective families, and here parents and "other" adults are likely to know and trust one another, making this transfer of intimacy perhaps more comfortable than it might be if the "others" were unknowns.

We know that the cultural patterns of these times lead us further and further into attitudes of individualism and lifestyles of isolation. With extended families scattered across the continent and beyond; with telecommuting replacing the social context of the office; with shopping malls replacing the local marketplace; and with neighborhoods characterized more by fences and alarms than by open doors and shared backyards, our experience of community is becoming rarer and rarer. To nurture the spirituality of children only within the family is to perpetuate the isolation of the family unit and to bypass one of the finest opportunities for community available to us.

Not every church or synagogue, to be sure, is a healthy, caring, supportive community. Not every religious education program is a loving, affirming, relevant and responsible program. But the imperfection of these institutions is no reason to avoid them. It is the responsibility of parents to seek out the religious communities that will best welcome and nurture both them as adults and their children. And then it is their continued responsibility to invest their energies in those communities to improve them where they need improving.

There is an upsurge of interest in spirituality presently swelling in our culture, but we must take careful note of the differences between religious community and some of these popular options. The proliferation of books, tapes, and seminars dealing with spiritual matters is often rooted more in commercialism than in faith.

It is in being together that attitudes and values are learned. It is in community that selves, souls, individuals are grown. It is in relationship, in being cherished, that we are both deepened and broadened.

I remember one sunny autumn Sunday afternoon when my children were in elementary school. We had been to church in the morning, of course, and they had brought friends home with them to have lunch and play through the afternoon. They were climbing trees in the woods behind our house, and in the exuberant energy of the day, full of the beauty of New England in the fall, full of the triumph of climbing to daring heights, full of the zest of childhood, their voices rang out with shouts and laughter and with song. And the song I heard from the treetops was,

"This little light of mine, I'm gonna let it shine.
This little light of mine, I'm gonna let it shine.
This little light of mine, I'm gonna let it shine,
Let it shine, let it shine, let it shine.

All around the neighborhood - - -
    All around this world of mine - - -
        I'm gonna let it shine"

It was the song they had sung in church school that morning, of course. They felt like singing and that was the piece fresh in their hearts and minds.

These same children Trick or Treated for UNICEF and not so many years later were demonstrating against military recruitment in their high school and for animal rights. They became outspoken and articulate on issues of gay rights and compassionate listeners when their friends were in trouble. They learned well to do justice, to love mercy, and to walk humbly with their God.

Epilogue

~

My colleague Reverend Gordon McKeeman tells this story:

> Our camper van is one of the less active members of the family. It does a great deal of "they also serve who only stand and wait" duty. It's reassuring to see it there ready to burst into activity at the turn of its key. The other day, though . . . I took to the van and turned the key. Nothing. Not a cough. Not a tremor. Not a flickering light. Nothing. Instant diagnosis—a dead battery. . . . Once the local AAA service had jolted the van's engine into action, and a new battery was installed, that should be the end of it. But, no, the minister has to use it as a parable.
>
> Many's the person who leaves his or her religion sitting idly in the corner ready to respond to an emergency—a crisis, accident, or untoward happening. . . . Comes the crisis. You leap to your religion and turn the key. Not a whimper, a cough or a shudder. Nothing. Possibly a little

preventive maintenance, a little more regular activity would have kept the battery charged and ready. That's one of the reasons that I like to go to church every Sunday—to keep my religion's pieces in working order. It's no accident that my mechanic says, "Run the car once a week"; and the minister says, "It'll keep your religion in good shape if you worship every Sunday."

It feels just a little shameless somehow for a minister to be advocating involvement in church community so vigorously. Although my own minister role makes it impossible for me to be a participant in the spiritual grounding of worship and church community in quite the same way that others are able to participate, still I am a part of the circle and can feel its power.

Several years ago I was able to participate in a spirituality group in my congregation. This group, called "In Touch," led in rotation by the several participants, was designed to evoke a sense of the spiritual. This was not a study group or a meditation group, although we occasionally did some meditating; it was designed to be an experiential program. We read stories in one another's hands and watched the sunset from a mountaintop in silence; we meditated on an orange and reflected on the history of each ingredient as we made bread; we chanted and listened to music in new ways.

From each session I returned to my daily routines with a heightened sense of the richness of life. I experienced a kind of opening that stayed with me. I was more alert, attentive, and sensitive; more mindful; more "in touch" with the natural world, my history, my body, my family; more in touch with patterns, relationships, and continuities. I was more expectant, and through this expectation I encountered greater beauty and love and sometimes a breathlessness and a quickening. I became more courageous and more compassionate. I think I became more faithful through those sessions, more filled with faith.

The spiritual dimension of life is available, awaiting our call, our attention, our presence. I have heard that there is a sign outside a Las Vegas gambling casino saying, "You must be present to win." We must be present. We must be mindful. We must have an openness and an expectancy to glimpses of the spirit. We must have a language, a story, a song, an image, available to express that which we glimpse. And, we must have a community to affirm and support the glimpses and experiences that will come, but that will dissipate if there are no arms to hold them, no sounding boards to bounce back their meanings.

In the lore of ancient China there is a story of a philosopher who was asked, "Where is the road called hope?" He replied, "It does not exist, but as people walk upon it, it comes into being." If we allow ourselves and our children to be limited by the secular bounds of our popular culture, we will not walk on the road. Our lack of belief, of faith, of connection to the larger-than-life will become a self-fulfilling prophecy. We will not be present. We, and our children, will not win, will not access the depth and richness that is available to us.

Those families who are cultivating the habit of church-going are giving their children a precious gift—a gift that enlivens their childhood and provides deep and sustaining roots for the future. The simple habit of churchgoing acknowledges that the spiritual life is of value and weaves connections to a web of faithful folks, connections to a religious community that can be life sustaining and life transforming.

Prayers, Meditations and Rituals

~

The following are samples of prayers and rituals that might be a part of family life. Please use them as prompters to create your own prayers for repeated, ritualistic use (daily, weekly, seasonally); for special events or needs as they arise; and to celebrate that which is most important in your family.

Great Spirit, fill us with light. Give us strength to understand and eyes to see. Teach us to walk the soft earth as relatives to all that live.

Sioux Prayer

To love while we live
And give help to each other
Is the sunshine of life
That turns night into day.

Rev. Lewis Latimer

Gestures and touch are often evocative for children, as in the following three examples:

May we have eyes that see, [touch eyes]
hearts that love, [touch chest]
and hands that are ready to serve, [extend hands]
for we would take our part as good neighbors in
this wide world [spread arms wide].

May I enter this day
with clear thoughts [touch forehead]
wise words [touch lips]
kind heart [place open palm over heart].

Let us hold hands quietly for a moment . . .
feeling love flow around us and through us,
knowing that as we give love away
there is always more within.

Table Graces

God, we thank you for this food,
for rest and home and all things good,
for wind and rain and sun above,
but most of all, for those we love.

unknown

Loving Spirit,
Be our guest,
Dine with us,
Share our bread,
That our table
Might be blessed
And our souls be fed.

Rev. Gary K. Kowalski

(can be sung to the tune of "Mary Had A Little Lamb")

The silver rain, the shining sun,
The fields where scarlet poppies run,
And all the ripples of the wheat
Are in the foods that we do eat.

So when we sit for every meal and
Say our grace, we always feel
That we are eating rain and sun
And fields where scarlet poppies run.

a Shaker grace

Bless our food,
Bless our friends,
Come, Spirit, be with us.
May our hearts fill with peace,
Let your presence surround us.
Spirit of Love may you bloom and grow,
Bloom and grow forever.

Bless our food,
Bless our friends,
Bless our lives forever.

Rev. Jan Evans-Tiller

(can be sung to the tune of "Edelweiss")

Candle Lightings

At mealtime, or for a quiet moment any time, a single candle might be lit, or multiple candles. Each member of the family could light a candle and/or speak one of the lines

This flame glows as light glows in the darkness.
This flame dances as growing things dance upon the green earth.
This flame flickers as life flickers for a precious while in each of us.
This flame is warm as the companionship of family and friends is warm.

Rev. Andrew M. Hill

We light this candle to remind ourselves to treat all people kindly because they are our brothers and sisters.

We light this candle to remind ourselves to take good care of the earth, because it is our home.

We light this candle to remind ourselves to live lives full of goodness and love, because that is how we will become the best we can be.

Teaching Prayer

If it is your hope that your children will not only experience prayer as created by you but will also learn to create their own, you will want to find ways for them to participate or ways for them to extend what you begin.

Here is a little morning prayer that could be begun in infancy. To begin the day, the parent, holding the child, might look out the window at the world outside (or step outdoors when that is possible) and say,

> The earth is good.
> Love is near.
> God is glad
> That you are here.

As the child learns to talk and to say the prayer for him or herself, it becomes,

> The earth is good.
> Love is near.
> God is glad
> That I am here.

Bedtime Moments

For an older child, you might begin a bedtime prayer in which you express your gratitude for the gifts of the day, and invite your child to add his or her listing of things for which they are thankful.

Sing "Twinkle, Twinkle Little Star," then say, "We are thankful for all wonderful and magical things—starlight and sunshine—life and love." On a cloudy or stormy night, you might say instead, "We know that there is beauty and magic in the world. Even when these are covered by clouds, we know they will return."

To say "I love you" to a child every night, no matter what has happened during the day, is an empowering, faith-nurturing ritual.

My friend Ruth Gibson says that when she had trouble sleeping, her mother drew a magic circle around her face, lightly touching her. It was a soothing ritual.

Lifting Up Significant Events

When a significant life passage, or an incident that feels either celebratory or disturbing, occurs, be creative in finding ways to bring to that moment the spiritual attention it deserves. When there is a success, a graduation, a milestone in growth (loss of first tooth, beginning menstruation), too often we rush to celebrate and miss the moment of pause to note in a deeper way the transformation that has occurred.

A hyped kind of celebration often overshadows the spiritual essence of birthdays, for instance. That one unique and precious life miraculously emerged out of the mystery—and that this one life grows and changes with every year—is worthy of a centered, prayerful ritual.

On the night before the child's birthday, gather the family together in a close circle or take some time at the child's bedside to light a candle and invite everyone to take a quiet moment to think about the past year in the child's life. Sometimes it's helpful to prompt such remembering by suggesting specific times and places (what happened this year in the summer, in the fall, etc.; what happened at the beach, at grandma's house, at school) for each one to recall silently. Then ask, "What were the happiest times this year?" The child should respond first, and then others can chime in. Continue with more questions:

"What has changed this year?" (home, school, new sibling, pets)

"How have you changed this year?"

"What have you learned?"

"Who has been really special to you or really helpful to you this year?"

"What do you like about yourself?"

"What do we all really like about you?"

"What are the new things you can look forward to in this next year?"

Invite everyone to sit quietly, breathe deeply, and be grateful for the year. After a moment, draw on what has just been said, and say something like,

> We are grateful for this year, with all its joys and its sorrows, its growth and change. We are grateful for Erin's laughter and kindness, for her bright paintings, and her special chocolate pudding. We look forward to this next year, to her growing taller, learning to play the recorder, riding to the park alone on her bike. No matter what the next year may bring, we will love and support her, and again next year there will be much for which to be thankful.

But it is not only the joyful times that need to be held in a spiritual way. Here are two examples of centering times for more difficult moments. For example, you can use this centering prayer when a child has experienced a failure:

> Let's sit for a minute and breathe deeply, feeling the air flow in—and out—in—and out—feeling the air move through our nostrils, drawing the air deeply in, way into our bellies, feeling that flow of life, that spark of life inside us.

From this place of calmness, talk for a few minutes with your child. Ask, "How are you feeling?" "Who do you feel you have let down?" "Is there anything you can do to change what happened?" Continue with the prayer:

> Let's pay attention to our breath again—in and out—in and out—draw deeply—as the breath goes deep into your center, bring your attention to the Spirit of Life that is within you, feel that flicker of energy, know that the Spirit of Life—within you and beyond you—is a spirit of love and acceptance and strength. Each breath is a new breath, but the love is always there, the acceptance is always there. Each breath is a new breath; the old one is gone; life goes on. What has happened now is over. Life goes on; love goes on. Life goes on; love goes on.

Sit quietly together for a time and then do something healing: Paint a picture, walk in the woods, listen to music, or eat ice cream.

If your child is in conflict with a friend, the following centering prayer may be helpful:

> We need to talk about why you and Jonathan are mad at each other. First, let's light a candle, then sit and take some deep breaths and soften our eyes.

Breathe deeply, feeling the air flowing through your nose, down into your chest, way down into your tummy.

Feel the air flow back out, as you feel your breath—in and out, in and out.

Feel how magical it is to be alive—how wonderful and how mysterious it is—to breathe—to feel—to feel love and happiness—also to feel sadness and even anger.

Clench your fists tightly for a moment and feel your anger. Open your fingers, hold your hands gently open and feel kindness.

Breathe deeply—way deep inside, further than your breath can go is the part of you that is Spirit (or holy, or God)—that Spirit is where your kindness comes from, the strongest, best part of you.

Breathe deeply—feel the warmth of kindness. Breathe deeply—feel the air, the life, flowing in and out—in and out.

Jonathan breathes in life too—in and out—breathes this same air and has a warm and holy place at his center. He's angry now too. His hands are clenched, but in time they will open again. Remember Jonathan's smile. Remember the times he's been kind to you, the good times you've had together.

Breathe deeply and remember how kind you can be.

Suggested Reading

~

For Parents:

Berends, Polly Berrien. *Gently Lead: How to Teach Your Children About God While Finding Out for Yourself.* Crossroad/Herder & Herder, 1998.

Carter, Stephen L. *Culture of Disbelief: How American Law and Politics Trivialize Religious Devotion.* Anchor, 1994.

Hahn, Thich Nhat. *The Miracle of Mindfulness: An Introduction to the Practice of Meditation.* Beacon Press, 1999.

Kushner, Harold. *When Children Ask About God: A Guide for Parents Who Don't Always Have All the Answers.* Schocken Books, 1995.

Nelson, Gertrud Mueller. *To Dance With God: Family Ritual and Community Celebration.* Paulist Press, 1987.

For Children:

Boritzer, Etan. *What Is God?* Firefly Books, 1990.

Frasier, Debra. *On the Day You Were Born: A Photo Journal.* Harcourt, 1995.

Sasso, Sandy Eisenberg. *In God's Name.* Jewish Lights Publishers, 1994.

Wood, Douglas. *Grandad's Prayers of the Earth.* Candlewick Press, 1999.

Wood, Douglas. *Old Turtle.* Scholastic Trade, 2001.

Many of these titles are available from the Unitarian Universalist Association Bookstore. Please call toll-free 1-800-215-9076 to order. For all other inquiries call (617) 742-2100, ext. 101 or see our website at http://www.uua.org/bookstore.